The Maximum Quantum Yield Controversy

The Maximum Quantum Yield Controversy

Otto Warburg and the "Midwest-Gang"

Kärin Nickelsen and Govindjee

Bern Studies in the History and Philosophy of Science

Nickelsen, Kärin:
The Maximum Quantum Yield Controversy – Otto Warburg and the
"Midwest-Gang" / Kärin Nickelsen and Govindjee – Bern, Bern Studies
in the History and Philosophy of Science (Bern Studies), 2011.

ISBN 978-3-9523421-9-0

Contents

ACKNOWLEDGMENTS

We are deeply grateful for the various forms of support we have received while working on this book. First, we thank the enormously engaged and helpful staff at the various archives that we consulted at the Max Planck Society (Germany), the Berlin-Brandenburg Academy of Sciences and Humanities (Germany), the University of Illinois at Urbana–Champaign (USA), the University of Chicago (USA), and the University of Cambridge (UK). Further, we thank all those who generously shared their memories and thoughts with us and contributed quotes and material; they are (in alphabetical order): Andrew A. Benson, Lars-Olof Björn, Jeanette Brown, Albert Frenkel, Howard Gest, Rajni Govindjee, Helen Arnold Herron, Geoffrey Hind, Ekkehard Höxtermann, Peter Homann, Miriam Jacob (Mauzerall), David Mauzerall, Burlyn Michel, David Walker and Colin Wraight.

Besides the University of Bern's History and Philosophy of Science Division (in the Institute of Philosophy) and the Department of Plant Biology at the University of Illinois at Urbana–Champaign, we would like to thank the following institutions for their generous financial support: The Young Academy at the Berlin-Brandenburg Academy of Sciences and Humanities and the German Academy of Sciences Leopoldina; the Hochschulstiftung of the Burgergemeinde Bern; and the Mittelbaufonds of the University of Bern. Materials that are presented in this little book were also included in the habilitation thesis of one of us (KN), which was submitted in 2009 to the Philosophisch-naturwissenschaftliche Fakultät (Department of Sciences) of the University of Bern, Switzerland. These parts of the text were edited by Margareta Simons (of Lucerne), which is gratefully acknowledged.

Govindjee is very thankful not only to his first photosynthesis mentor Robert (Bob) Emerson for training him in the art and science of manometry, in particular for measuring quantum yields of photosynthesis, but also to his second mentor Eugene Rabinowitch for teaching him how to think and communicate. Kärin Nickelsen is particularly grateful to Gerd Graßhoff, head of the University of Bern's History and Philosophy of Science Division.

Kärin Nickelsen
History and Philosophy of Science; University of Bern/Switzerland

Govindjee
Plant Biology, Biochemistry and Biophysics & Computational Biology
University of Illinois at Urbana–Champaign/USA

Chapter I

INTRODUCTION

Photosynthesis is the conversion of solar energy into biochemically usable forms of energy, which are then employed to produce carbohydrates, while molecular oxygen is released. Finding out how this process is accomplished in plants and algae was one of the major research challenges of the twentieth century. While the 1920s saw the first substantial advances in elucidating the process, it was only in the 1950s that, based on new spectroscopic techniques as well as on the sophisticated use of carbon-14 as a radioactive tracer molecule, molecular models were developed that we still consider basically correct today.[1]

Whoever turns to the history of photosynthesis research in the twentieth century is soon confronted with the fact that this exciting period from 1920 to 1960 was in large part overshadowed by a bitter controversy in which most of the leading scientists in the field were involved. It centered on the question, how efficient the process of photosynthesis was. To put it in quantitative terms, the question was, how many light quanta were minimally required to release one molecule of oxygen; or, its inverse, how many oxygen molecules were maximally released through the effect of one light quantum.[2] This question was brought into the field by the the

---

[1]For an introduction into how photosynthesis works, see Blankenship (2002). For treatments of the history of photosynthesis research in otherwise specialized books, see, e.g., the pertinent sections in Rabinowitch (1945) and Loomis (1960). Photosynthesis is also touched upon in general works on the history of biochemistry, such as, e.g., in Fruton (1999) (pp. 325–329), although the main focus there is on animal and human metabolism. For timelines and surveys specifically of the history of photosynthesis research, see, e.g., Myers (1974), Höxtermann (1992), Huzisige & Ke (1993), Gest & Blankenship (2004), Govindjee & Krogmann (2004) and Nickelsen (2008b). The work of Govindjee (one name only) deserves special mention: he has been promoting studies in the history of photosynthesis research for many decades now and he played a pivotal role in introducing a "Historical Corner" in the journal *Photosynthesis Research*, in which tributes, obituaries, minireviews and personal perspectives are published. Together with Howard Gest, Thomas Beatty and John Allen, Govindjee edited, in the early years of the twenty-first century, three issues *Photosynthesis Research* that were entirely dedicated to the history of the subject; see Vols. 73 (2002), 76 (2003) and 80 (2004). The papers in these issues have more recently been collated into a seminal volume entitled "Discoveries in Photosynthesis"; see Govindjee, Beatty, Gest & Allen (2005). Nickelsen (2009b) provides a narrative of the history of photosynthesis research from ca. 1840 to 1960 as well as an analysis of the scientists' heuristic strategies.

[2]See, e.g., Rabinowitch & Govindjee (1969) for an introduction into quantum yield measurements and their role in photosynthesis research.

German cell physiologist Otto Warburg (1883–1970). Together with his long-standing collaborator Erwin Negelein (1897–1979), Warburg found, in 1923, that a minimum value of 4 to 5 quanta of light was required to produce one molecule of photosynthetic oxygen.[3] Determining this figure was highly valuable because once it was known how much energy in terms of light quanta photosynthesis required it became much easier to reconstruct its pathway: many of the possible alternatives looked far less attractive than before when it was found that they did not fit the determined energy budget. At that time, it was already known from the work of the English plant physiologist Frederick Frost Blackman (1866–1947), published as Blackman (1905), that the rate of photosynthesis first increases linearly with light intensity, whereas at some point it attains saturation. Hence, the yield of photosynthesis (measured from the slope of the rate of oxygen evolution against light intensity) is higher at low light intensities, which implies that at these light intensities the quantum requirement is lower. It is, in fact, only the lowest number of quanta required for the evolution of one molecule of oxygen that was of theoretical importance: According to Albert Einstein's (1879–1955) Law of Photochemical Equivalence of 1912, only from this value conclusions could be drawn as to the number of photochemical steps involved and to the amount of energy necessary to make the process operate.[4]

Hence, the minimum quantum requirement (or, its inverse, the maximum quantum yield) of photosynthesis was regarded by most of the photosynthesis experts working in the 1920s and 1930s as a vital piece of information. The 1923 Warburg–Negelein value of 4 to 5 quanta was generally accepted, and it remained virtually unchallenged until the end of the 1930s. Not only did the experiments appear well-founded and the results conclusive (which was hardly surprising, considering that Warburg was renowned for his exceptional skill in conducting experiments), but the value of around 4 light quanta per molecule of oxygen also nicely matched theoretical expectations: The conversion of water and carbon dioxide into molecular oxygen and a moiety of carbohydrate required a minimum calculated energy input of 112 kilocalories (kcal), while red light, which was known to be the most efficient region in the spectrum for bringing about photosynthesis, carried about 40 kcal per light quantum. Thus, at 100 % efficiency of the process, photosynthesis would require 2.8 light quanta per oxygen molecule; and since no process could possibly run at total efficiency, a value slightly higher than this was to be expected. The value of 4, furthermore, seemed to be highly significant to many

---

[3]These values were published in Warburg & Negelein (1922) and Warburg & Negelein (1923).

[4]See Einstein (1912a), Einstein (1912b).

photosynthesis researchers, because it corresponded so neatly to the 4 hydrogen atoms (or, alternatively, electrons) that had to change their places and bondings in the process of turning carbon dioxide (CO_2) into the basic element of carbohydrates (CH_2O). Yet, however well all this fitted together, a quantum requirement of 4 to 5 was still so close to the theoretical limit given by the calculation above that it was extremely difficult to devise a model of the mechanism that could convincingly explain the relevant empirical findings.

In view of the importance of quantum efficiencies, it is not surprising that in the second half of the 1930s research groups at the University of Wisconsin, Madison, at the University of Chicago, and at the Carnegie Institution of Washington at Stanford started to re-examine the question independently, which quickly resulted in serious concerns being raised about the validity of Warburg and Negelein's values. In fact, they were increasingly questioned – most vigorously by one of Warburg's former doctoral students Robert Emerson (1903–1959), together with several of his co-workers, who criticized the methods that Warburg and Negelein had applied. In agreement with the research group at the University of Wisconsin at Madison, Emerson argued that 8 to 12 light quanta were needed for photosynthesis. Papers and arguments were exchanged, but no agreement reached, which led Emerson to invite Warburg to come to his laboratory at the University of Illinois at Urbana–Champaign in 1948. (The meeting was displayed in the form of a cartoon published in a 1948 newsletter of the then Botany Department of the University of Illinois at Urbana–Champaign; see Figure I.1.) The original idea was that the two researchers would compare their experimental protocols and thereby settle the disconcerting discrepancies that had arisen: disconcerting, because both Emerson and Warburg were renowned for their mastery of manometry. Both used the same technique and the same organism – indeed, Emerson had been trained by Warburg; yet they obtained data that differed by a factor of two or three.[5]

However, Warburg's stay in Urbana proved unfruitful: nothing was settled and the two opponents parted as enemies. Consequently, the controversy continued to grow during the 1950s – to such an extent that the biophysicist Roderick Clayton commented, in 1965, that "the quantum efficiency of photosynthesis became perhaps the most exhaustively measured phenomenon in the history of science".[6] It was only in the 1960s, when models including two different light-reactions became accepted in photosynthesis, that the issue was considered settled in favor

---

[5]Cf. the account of this episode in Rabinowitch (1961).
[6]Clayton (1965), p. 40.

of the higher quantum requirement, although Warburg never accepted this solution.[7]

The story of this controversy has been told many times, in historical papers, personal perspectives, tributes, obituaries and reviews.[8] In this little book, we will examine the controversy in more historical detail and draw several perspectives together. Based on previously unknown archival sources, we shall try to reconstruct and explain the course of events and analyze the arguments, brought forward by the two parties. In doing so, we shall concentrate on the first culmination of the debate, when Warburg came to the United States. At this time, Emerson and others were still truly interested in a constructive exchange of viewpoints, aiming at a benevolent solution, while Warburg's intentions are not so clear.

In order to gain a better understanding of this episode, it is important to consider three issues head on. *First*, the question of the maximum quantum yield was an extremely important one. It was not an arbitrary number that was under debate, but one of the key parameters, on which all modeling of the photosynthesis mechanism had to be based. Thus, the keen interest in finding the true value was well founded. *Second*, the debate was not a fictitious one. The experimental difficulties people faced were enormous: one had to be extremely meticulous when measuring the quantum yields of life processes. The greatest difficulty was the impossibility to clearly differentiate between gas exchanges caused by photosynthesis and gas exchanges caused by respiration. This was a serious problem, and although all protagonists acknowledged its existence, they were unable to deal with it in an appropriate manner. *Third*, the efficiency of photosynthesis is strongly dependent on several factors. It is only at very low light intensities that the system approaches its maximum efficiency. This means that all sorts of quantum yields can be accurately measured, while these may not be the maximum quantum yields. Hence, all data were in principle open to criticism and people had to look for convincing criteria to establish their plausibility. Which these were, and how the opposing party countered them is of great interest, both for the history and the philosophy of science.

---

[7]For an account of how the two-light-reaction models developed in the 1960s see, e.g., Govindjee & Björn (2011) and Nickelsen (2009*b*), Chapter VI. See also Duysens (1989) for his perspective as well as Witt (1991).

[8]The controversy and its consequences are mentioned, e.g., in many of the contributions to Govindjee et al. (2005).

Figure I.1: A cartoon depicting the controversy on the minimum quantum requirement of photosynthesis between Robert Emerson (left; 12 quanta/oxygen) and Otto Warburg (right; 4 quanta/oxygen). In the center is shown Eugene Rabinowitch attempting to bring the two sides closer. Source: A 1948 newsletter of the then Botany Department of the University of Illinois at Urbana–Champaign, Illinois.

Chapter II

THE STANDARD VALUE AND THE PROTAGONISTS UP TO 1948

1 THE STANDARD VALUE OF 1923

Otto Warburg (1883–1970) was one of the most successful and influential cell physiologists of the twentieth century (see Figure II.1 for a portrait).[1] He was born into a middle-class German family of partly Jewish origin, while his father was the experimental physicist Emil Warburg (1846–1931), himself one of the most eminent scientists of his time. Otto Warburg first decided to study chemistry; yet, after having received his PhD in 1906, he chose to broaden his education by studying medicine. After a Doctor of Medicine (1911) and his habilitation (1912), Warburg began his studies of the processes of cell oxidation – a research theme that continued to fascinate him for his entire career. It was largely because of Warburg's work in this field that he was awarded the Nobel Prize in Medicine or Physiology in 1931.

Otto Warburg embarked upon research in the field of photosynthesis in 1918, after he came back from his military service in the First World War.[2] He entered the field with two closely related articles, published as Warburg (1919) and Warburg (1920), in which he dealt with the general mechanism of the process.[3] It was in these papers that Warburg introduced a number of new techniques that were quickly to become standard procedures in photosynthesis research and remained so until the 1970s. These included the use of manometric rather than gasometric or titrimetric methods for measuring the rate and progress of photosynthesis. (See Figures II.2 and II.3 for drawings of Warburg's manometric apparatus.) To fully exploit the advantages of this new technique, War-

---

[1] For general accounts of Otto Warburg's life and work, see, e.g., Krebs (1979), Henning (1987), Höxtermann & Sucker (1989), Werner (1991) and Höxtermann (2001); see also the biography of Warburg provided on the Official Web Site of the Nobel Prize at http://nobelprize.org/nobel_prizes/medicine/laureates/1931/warburg-bio.html. Selected parts of Warburg's sister's personal notes, including her personal perspective on Otto, were published in Rüskamp (1989). Warburg's contribution to the theory of cell respiration, as reflected in his correspondence with, e.g., the physiologists Jacques Loeb, Leonor Michaelis and Otto Meyerhof, is treated in Werner (1996), while Kohler (1973) investigates the background of Warburg's concept of the "Atmungsferment". On Warburg's experimental methods in photosynthesis, see also Hoppe (1997), pp. 19–20.

[2] For an analysis of how Warburg came to photosynthesis research, see Nickelsen (2009a).

[3] For an analysis of these first contributions by Warburg to photosynthesis research, see, e.g., Nickelsen (2007) and Höxtermann (2007).

Figure II.1: Otto Warburg around 1920. (Reproduced from Krebs (1979), Figure 2.)

burg also replaced the use of leaves and whole plants as test organisms with the unicellular green alga *Chlorella*, which to this day is a well-known model organism in photosynthesis research.[4] In addition, Warburg also employed sophisticated photophysical techniques, which most biologists at the time never had heard of, such as bolometry, absorption measurement and intermittent illumination by means of rotating sectors.

To complement his model of the photosynthesis mechanism, Warburg carried out, together with his long-standing collaborator Erwin Negelein (1897–1979), an investigation into the efficiency of the process, the results of which were published as Warburg & Negelein (1922) and Warburg & Negelein (1923). In their experiments, Warburg and Negelein exposed *Chlorella* cells to light of wavelengths between 570 and 645 nm, that is, from yellow to orange-red light. In order to get a reliable value for the amount of absorbed energy, Warburg and Negelein used very thick algae suspensions, so that practically all the incident light on the suspension was absorbed. Photosynthesis was measured manometrically, with the measured oxygen release as the indicator of the process's rate.

The results of the study Warburg & Negelein (1922) included the important finding that the efficiency of photosynthesis was highly dependent on the conditions under which the algae had been cultivated: the highest

---

[4]See Zallen (1993) for a thoughtful discussion about the use of *Chlorella* (and other algae) as model organisms in photosynthesis research.

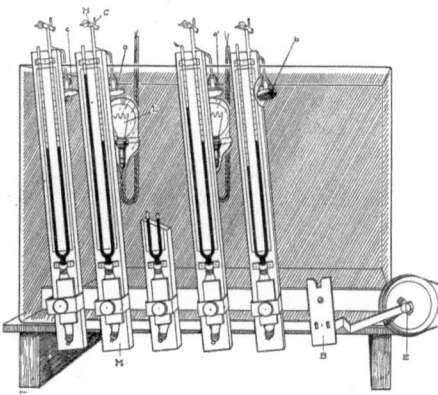

Figure II.2: A drawing of Warburg's complete measuring apparatus (which became known as "Warburg apparatus"). The manometers are mounted on a thermostat, so that the vessels can be illuminated with light bulbs from below. A v-belt connected to an electric motor, part of which can be seen on the right of the illustration, oscillates the manometers. (Reproduced from Warburg (1919), p. 245.)

efficiency was achieved with cells that had been transferred to low light intensities after having grown for some time in high light intensities. The efficiency measurements themselves revealed that, on average, an extremely high percentage of between 60 and 70 % of the absorbed radiation energy could be transformed into chemical energy. Warburg and Negelein drew attention to the fact that, due to their experimental set-up and their measuring process, the measured values should be considered too low, and that the actual efficiency might be even higher. However, in Warburg & Negelein (1923) the efficiency value was slightly reduced to an average (in red light) of 59 % efficiency, while the maximum value they had been able to achieve in 1923 was 63.5 % efficiency – which was still a very high figure. This was due to a change in the procedure they used: while in 1922, Warburg and Negelein had determined the chemical work effected by one calorie of absorbed radiation by extrapolating from values at higher light intensities, in 1923 they reconsidered this procedure, since, as they conceded, it was not known which curve the extrapolation should be made to follow. Instead, they measured the efficiency in the lowest possible light intensities, and when no significant increase in value was found, they assumed that this value was the limiting case.

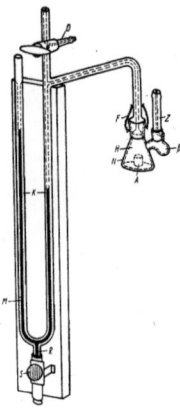

Figure II.3: A drawing of a manometer used by Otto Warburg in his photosynthesis experiments. The manometer vessel that holds the suspension of algae is shown on the right. (Reproduced from Warburg (1926), p. 1.)

These were spectacular findings. Very few people had so far tried to transfer the approach of quantum yield measurements to the study of photosynthesis. An earlier estimate of the efficiency of photosynthesis had been provided in 1905 by two English plant physiologists, Horace T. Brown (1848–1925) and Francis Escombe, who found a maximum efficiency of photosynthesis of only 6 % – which was clearly much lower than Warburg and Negelein's values.[5] Warburg and Negelein sharply criticized the earlier efficiency experiments and found Brown and Escombe's conclusions to be invalid since, in this earlier study, light absorbance was measured by weakening of light passing through the leaf, and, thus, the light scattered by the leaf must have been erroneously read as absorption.

As mentioned earlier, the efficiency of photosynthesis was particularly interesting in view of the ongoing search for the underlying mechanism of the process. A simple calculation revealed that reducing one molecule of carbonic acid to the level of carbohydrates required, at the very least, an energy input of 112 kcal. From this, it followed that, on average, the carbonic acid had to interact with at least three pigment molecules, if each of them absorbed one red light quantum with an average energy of 49 kcal each. Although Warburg and Negelein did not yet dare to draw any concrete inferences from their finding, they did emphasize that in view of the high overall efficiency of the process, the reduction of carbonic acid had to be straightforward, that is, without the inclusion

_____
[5]H. T. Brown & Escombe (1905).

of many intermediate reactions that would require additional energy. Possibly, Warburg and Negelein thought in 1922, a formic acid peroxide was formed, which then, via a formaldehyde stage, would yield glucose in a condensation reaction – this was the pathway which the German chemist Richard Willstätter (1872–1942) had suggested in 1918, together with his collaborator Arthur Stoll (1887–1971).[6]

The reception of these papers by Warburg and Negelein was highly favorable; and the requirement of 4-5 light quanta per molecule of oxygen was regarded as the authoritative answer to the question of photosynthetic efficiency for the next fifteen years.

2   First Opponents of the Warburg–Negelein Value

William A. Arnold and Microcalorimetry

The first of the several researchers, whose data on the maximum quantum yield of photosynthesis was in disagreement with that of Warburg–Negelein's value, was William A. Arnold (1904–2001). (See Arnold's photograph in Figure II.4.) In 1932, Arnold had collaborated with Robert Emerson in the experiments which gave birth to the idea of the existence of a "photosynthetic unit", in which more than 2000 molecules of chlorophyll cooperated. Four years later, in 1936, this idea was conceptually elaborated by Hans Gaffron (1902–1979) and Kurt Wohl (1896–1962).[7] Thereafter, Arnold had followed Emerson's recommendation and moved from the California Institute of Technology (Caltech) to Harvard University, where he entered the graduate program in General Physiology. Part of Arnold's project was to measure the minimum quantum requirement of photosynthetic oxygen, and in order to carry this out Arnold developed microcalorimetric techniques, which were quite different from Warburg's manometry: In microcalorimetry, the process is not monitored by registering pressure changes but by determining the resulting heat in a leaf or

---

[6]See Warburg & Negelein (1922), p. 249. Together with Stoll, Willstätter had published in 1918 an influential monograph on photosynthesis, see Willstätter & Stoll (1918). In 1915, Willstätter was awarded the Nobel Prize in Chemistry "for his researches on plant pigments, especially chlorophyll". Note, however, that the reduction of carbon dioxide to carbohydrates via the stage of formaldehyde was not originally Willstätter's idea but a very popular assumption at the time. For an analysis of this suggestion, which goes back to the German chemist Adolf von Baeyer (1835–1917), and its long and successful history of reception, see Nickelsen (2009b), Chapter I, as well as (with a more philosophical focus) Nickelsen & Graßhoff (in press, 2011).

[7]For the publication of the experimental results, see Emerson & Arnold (1932); Arnold (1991) provides an autobiographical perspective on how these experiments were conducted. See Govindjee, Amesz & Knox (1996a) for further information on Arnold; note therein, e.g., the contribution by Arnold's daughter, Helen A. Herron (1996). The conceptual elaboration of the "photosynthetic unit" was given in Gaffron & Wohl (1936); on Gaffron, see, e.g., Homann (2005).

Figure II.4: William Arnold as a young man: This is a photograph taken in 1922 at his High School graduation time. (Courtesy of Helen A. Herron.)

a cell suspension. By this means, Arnold found that a minimum number of 8 light quanta were required to produce one molecule of oxygen during photosynthesis. Although the number 8 was two times greater than the Warburg–Negelein value of 4, it seems that Arnold assumed at the time that 8 was low enough to be included in the same range. This would explain why he did not emphasize the difference and publish them in a research paper.[8]

Arnold's results were published much later, in Arnold (1949), and, as he stated in this paper, only at the insistence of Gaffron, who had assured Arnold that his quantum yield values had become important in view of the developing controversy on the subject. (See Gaffron's photograph in Figure II.5.) Yet, even then, Arnold did not mention that the maximum quantum yield that he had measured differed from that of Warburg and Negelein – Arnold still believed that he had confirmed Warburg and Negelein's finding of an extremely low quantum requirement, so that there was no need to discuss the question any further. The dry summary of Arnold's findings, therefore, reads: *"In no case did the number of quanta used per CO_2 molecule reduced fall below nine"*.[9] This was characteristic of Arnold's general attitude to putting his results into

---

[8]See Arnold (1935) for the PhD thesis, submitted in 1935 to Harvard University, Cambridge, Massachusetts.

[9]Arnold (1949), p. 276.

Figure II.5: Hans Gaffron (left) with James Franck (middle); the person on the right is unidentified. (Photograph taken in 1951, at the University of Chicago; it was provided by the family of Hans Gaffron through Peter Homann and published before as Figure 2 in Homann (2005).)

print: Although Arnold contributed greatly to photosynthesis research as well as many other scientific areas, he was always reluctant to publish his findings. Indeed, Arnold is remembered for having said that scientific results should be engraved in stone: he believed that, faced with such a formidable task, scientists would be much more discerning about what was publicized; hence, publications would become more worthy.[10]

THE RESEARCH TEAM FROM THE UNIVERSITY OF WISCONSIN, MADISON

Around the same time as Arnold, an interdisciplinary research team at the University of Wisconsin at Madison, also started to re-evaluate the quantum yield requirement. This team included the plant physiologists Winston M. Manning (1910–2002, John F. Stauffer and Benjamin M. Duggar (1872–1956) as well as the renowned photochemist Farrington Daniels (1889–1972). In 1938, they presented the first published challenge to Warburg and Negelein's quantum yield value, as Manning, Stauffer,

---

[10]Cf. Govindjee, Knox & Amesz (1996*b*), p. 1; Govindjee, Allen & Beatty (2004).

Duggar & Daniels (1938). For their experiments, the group had developed a (rather cumbersome) chemical gas analysis method, which they applied to *Chlorella* cells. By this means, they had arrived at a minimum quantum requirement of 16 to 20 per molecule of oxygen evolved – diverging from Warburg's value by a factor of four or five. With hindsight it is clear that many of their experiments were not in the range where minimum quantum requirement ought to be measured (namely, at very low light intensities). However, this publication caused quite a stir in the photosynthesis research collective, which was reinforced when a year later the group published new results, in Magee, de Witt, Smith & Daniels (1939), based on microcalorimetric techniques: the findings suggested that 12 light quanta were required to produce one molecule of oxygen. Out of the seventeen experiments that they conducted, ten gave a value of approximately 10 quanta per molecule of oxygen evolved. The authors also recognized that some of their own earlier experiments with higher values were incorrect.

FOSTER F. RIEKE

Quantum yields of photosynthesis were also measured in the late 1930s by the physicist Foster F. Rieke (1905–1970), who at the time was James Franck's (1882–1964) assistant at Johns Hopkins University in Baltimore, Maryland. Rieke (1939) presented the first results of this project. Therein, Rieke explicitly stated (p. 238) that the results of the group based in Madison as well as other *"unpublished reports"*, which were not specified, had prompted him to undertake this research. Rieke had decided to use Warburg's own manometric techniques in order to discover whether he could duplicate the original findings. In this Rieke succeeded, as he arrived at an average value of about 5 quanta for the minimum requirement: a fair confirmation of Warburg–Negelein. However, Rieke found that the values strangely varied according to the method of calculation, which led him to conclude that *"either there is an obscure systematic error in one method of measurement or, under the conditions of the experiments, photosynthesis and respiration do not follow a simple course"* (p. 243). It is worth pointing out, for reasons that will be clear later, that Rieke obtained his lowest figures only when he used a phosphate-containing medium for the cell suspension, following the recipe of the biochemist Dean Burk (1904–1988), who was also working at Johns Hopkins at the time and whose help was acknowledged in Rieke's paper.[11] On only one occasion did Rieke use a carbonate-bicarbonate buffer solution, in which

---

[11]Burk became famous thanks to his 1934 paper co-authored with the physical chemist Hans Lineweaver (1907–2009), in which the famous Lineweaver–Burk plot method is introduced; see Lineweaver & Burk (1934).

he measured a minimum requirement of about 8 quanta: *"The quantum efficiency was reduced [to] 40%,"* Rieke stated in view of this aberrant run, while he surmised that some property of the buffer solution must have been responsible for this diverging value.[12] From Rieke's correspondence with Franck at the time, one can see that the latter found these low values satisfactory. On 29 July 1938, Franck wrote to his assistant:

> *I agree entirely to each remark you make and I am also very content with the result that the quantum yield is between 1/4.5 and 1/5. I think there is no sense in going on further and I am pretty convinced that the publication of the results will find great interest among the people working in that field.*[13]

Later correspondence shows, however, that Rieke nevertheless intended to continue with his studies. In his 1939 paper, for instance, Rieke pointed to the fact that it would be desirable *"that methods be introduced which [would] avoid as far as possible a large correction for respiration, and such experiments are being undertaken by the author"* (p. 239). Yet, this further research never materialized – even though Franck continued to probe Rieke on his work. In 1942, Franck even turned to Mrs. Rieke for help in securing the paper, pleading that it did not matter if it was not entirely finished: *"If only the actual results are in it, we can add some 'gravy and potatoes' to the 'main course' and send it back to you, and if Foster doesn't like our additions, he may throw them out."* To which Franck added: *"I think we just have to publish that paper soon; otherwise, Foster's whole efforts throughout several years may be in vain."*[14] Nonetheless, despite a number of ever more pressing requests from Franck, it was only in 1949 that Rieke's data of the years 1939 to 1941 saw the light of the day.[15] The result of Rieke's prolonged efforts was that, according to his experiments, *"a preponderance of evidence indicates that the maximum efficiency lies between the limits 0.09 and 0.11, and that there is no unequivocal evidence that it is appreciably greater than 0.12"* (p. 270). Or, put in another way, the minimum quantum requirement for photosynthesis as measured by Rieke was 9 to 12.

---

[12] Rieke (1939), p. 243; see also Table IV. p. 242.

[13] Franck to Rieke on 29 July 1938. Franck, James. Papers, [Box 7, Folder 9], Special Collections Research Center, University of Chicago Library.

[14] Franck to Mrs Rieke on 9 May 1942. Franck, James. Papers, [Box 7, Folder 9], Special Collections Research Center, University of Chicago Library.

[15] See Rieke (1949); several factors may have contributed to the delay in publication; in addition to other distractions, Rieke's involvement in war-time work with the Magnetron Group of the Massachusetts Institute of Technology (MIT) Radiation Laboratory in Cambridge, was most probably a cause.

In the meantime, another major protagonist had entered the stage. Already in his 1939 paper, Rieke had acknowledged that, in a lecture given at a symposium on photochemistry at Stanford University in August 1938, the plant physiologist and biophysicist Robert Emerson had criticized the methods used by Warburg and Negelein. On 20 July 1939, Emerson turned directly to Rieke, in response to the latter's paper of April of that year, in which the value of 5 had been published. Emerson wrote that his group had arrived at the same low quantum requirement values as Rieke, but only when they had used a very specific medium for the cells:

> *When we tried to repeat them [the experiments] using the medium, which you specified, we were unsuccessful. Thinking that you had probably followed Warburg & Negelein in using tap water, we sent to Baltimore for some tap water, and with this we were at once able to duplicate your results.*

And then Emerson added the following lines, which included the stunning announcement that he had obtained a quantum yield of 3, which would have implied an efficiency of almost 100 %:

> *We are preparing some of our results for publication, and including a description of a medium in glass-distilled water in which we can regularly produce cells giving quantum yields of about 3 quanta per CO_2. We think it should be easy to duplicate these results in other laboratories by following a more standardizing technique. If you care to try out our medium, I shall be glad to send you a full description of it in advance of publication.[16]*

3   EMERSON AND LEWIS'S CHALLENGE

Robert Emerson (1903–1959) dedicated his entire professional career to the study of photosynthesis with manometric methods; and his findings profoundly influenced and promoted this field of research.[17] (See Figure II.6 for a photograph of Emerson.) Having received his Bachelor of Science degree at Harvard in 1925, Emerson continued his graduate work in the country that was then the center of science: Germany, where Emerson concluded his education, in 1927, with a PhD awarded by the Friedrich Wilhelm University, Berlin – although the work had been done in Otto Warburg's division at the Berlin-based Kaiser Wilhelm

---

[16]Emerson to Rieke on 20 July 1939. Franck, James. Papers, [Box 7, Folder 9], Special Collections Research Center, University of Chicago Library. Emphasis copied from the original letter.

[17]For biographical information on Emerson, see Rabinowitch (1959), Rabinowitch (1961), Govindjee (2001) and Govindjee (2004).

Figure II.6: Robert Emerson at his desk in the Natural History Building at the University of Illinois at Urbana. (Photograph taken by Govindjee in 1957.)

Institute for Biology. Emerson then returned to Harvard, until, in 1930, he took up the post of Assistant Professor of Biophysics at the Caltech in Pasadena, California. Emerson only left Caltech when, in 1946, he was made Research Professor of Botany at the University of Illinois at Urbana–Champaign as well as the director of the Photosynthesis Project there (see below, Section 5, p. 37).

It is not entirely clear at which point Emerson began to doubt the validity of the Warburg–Negelein experiments. Although he was still convinced of Warburg's efficiency values in 1932, five years later, in 1937, Emerson embarked on an extended project to revisit the quantum yield question. He took a leave of absence from Caltech, and spent two years at the Plant Biology Laboratory of the Carnegie Institution of Washington (on the campus of Stanford University). Emerson was the guest of the plant physiologist Herman A. Spoehr (1885–1954), author of one of the first monographs on photosynthesis, and he was also able to benefit from working with the skilled physicist Charlton M. Lewis (1905–1996). Very soon Emerson found that there might be more problems than Warburg and Negelein had acknowledged. In addition to the type of water used, which Emerson had discussed with Rieke, there was a curious induction period, which upset the manometrical vessel constant at the onset of illumination and thus was a substantial confounding factor to the measurements. Furthermore, Emerson was concerned about the handling of the bolometer; he believed that Warburg might not have operated it correctly, since Warburg used the instrument in a position that differed from the position in which these instruments were usually calibrated. This implied, so Emerson wrote, that they risked having a measuring error of about 10 % (which for Emerson, who tried to find out whether 4 or 5 light quanta per molecule oxygen were necessary, was important).[18] Finally, Emerson had found that, during transition from light to dark and vice versa, the gas exchanges had strong oscillations, which he was not yet able to explain. Emerson did not foresee the enormous consequences of his findings; however, a year later, in December 1939, Emerson was adamant that the values reported by Warburg and Negelein were incorrect. On a Christmas card to Warburg, he wrote:

> I shall send you a reprint in January, because I believe you will be interested in our results. The [maximum quantum] yield really is not as high as you and Negelein thought.[19]

THE CARBON DIOXIDE BURST (1939–41)

The article Emerson had alluded to in his Christmas card was published as Emerson & Lewis (1939): "Factors influencing the efficiency of photosynthesis". In this paper, Emerson and Lewis systematically explored the external factors that influenced the photosynthetic yield. They demonstrated that this value was strongly dependent not only on the type of water used but also on the addition of certain heavy metals, light conditions during the growth of algae, the age of the culture and the wavelength of light at which the algae were grown. Keeping the cultures at lower temperatures also tended to increase photosynthetic efficiency. Thus, the whole issue transpired to be far more complicated than had previously been thought. However, under conditions that seemed optimal, and otherwise following Warburg's experimental protocol, Emerson and Lewis arrived at the surprising yield of 0.33 molecules of oxygen released per absorbed light quantum – that is, a minimum quantum requirement of no more than 3! (This was the value that Emerson had indicated to Rieke in his letter of 1938; see quote above.) However, Emerson & Lewis (1939) did not believe that this value, which was beyond all theoretical expectations, really reflected the efficiency of photosynthesis. They rather suggested that these exceedingly high values were an artifact of the technique. The decisive source of error was identified as being the curious gas exchange effects that appeared whenever the light source was turned on or off. They wrote:

---

[18]Cf. Archive of the Berlin-Brandenburg Academy of Sciences and Humanities (BBAW), NL Warburg 262. Emerson to Warburg, 5 Nov. 1938.

[19]Archive of the BBAW, NL Warburg 262. Emerson to Warburg, Dec. (Christmas) 1939.

With our improved technique we found that after a change from light to dark, or vice versa, the rate of pressure change was subject to large deviations before coming to the new steady value. [...] When the light is turned on, a sharp increase of pressure occurs at once and lasts from two to five minutes. Under some circumstances the maximum rate attained may be two or three times the steady rate in the light (the respiration correction being included in each case). [...] When the light is turned off, the rate of pressure change returns approximately to its former (negative) value for a few minutes but then shows an increase. The maximum is reached in about seven minutes and may be 20 per cent above the steady rate, which is regained after 10 to 20 minutes.[20]

Emerson and Lewis were persuaded that these deviations were due to changes in the ratio between oxygen and carbon dioxide; in fact, the sudden peak after the onset of illumination was caused mainly by the evolution of carbon dioxide. The authors concluded, rather succinctly: *"This implies that for the short periods of darkness and illumination used for efficiency measurements the assumptions on which photosynthesis is computed from pressure changes become incorrect."* (p. 815). This last sentence effectively dismissed all previous quantum yield determinations, all of which had depended on the premise that the ratio CO_2/O_2 during photosynthesis, denoted by γ ("gamma"), was unity. Warburg & Negelein (1923) had attempted to double-check this assumption, and found the ratio to be -0.9; yet they had arrived at this value at high light intensities and from measurements carried out over a period of time of more than one hour. Emerson & Lewis (1939) strongly suspected that the value obtained under these conditions did not hold for low light intensities and shorter periods of illumination – that is, for the conditions used in the actual quantum yield experiments. Thus, they summarized their conclusion:

In view of the apparent variability of γ disclosed by our results, measurements made in this way cannot be accepted as significant until the method has been applied in such a way as to permit the simultaneous determination of both carbon dioxide and oxygen exchange.[21]

Two years later, Emerson and Lewis made a new attempt to determine quantum yields, published as Emerson & Lewis (1941). In this

---

[20]Emerson & Lewis (1939), pp. 814–815. They also discussed the problem of respiration changes from dark to light, yet discarded this possibility as insufficient to account for the magnitude of the error involved.

[21]Emerson & Lewis (1939), pp. 817.

paper, the "two-vessel method" was introduced, which enabled the exchange of oxygen and carbon dioxide to be measured simultaneously, so that the ratio between these two variables could be controlled. The trick was to use two manometer vessels containing the same quantity of identical algal suspensions, which, however, had different gas-to-liquid ratios. This enabled the calculation of the exchange of carbon dioxide and the exchange of oxygen independently of each other. By this means, Emerson and Lewis were now in a position to trace the development of the ratio CO_2/O_2, that is, γ, in quantum yield measurements, without simply assuming its constancy. Their findings fully justified the tentative objections raised in 1939: The value of γ was extremely unstable, with the greatest variation taking place in the first ten minutes of light or darkness (that is, in the exact time slot that Warburg and Negelein had used for their readings). Emerson and Lewis concluded that this was the cause of a considerable systematic error in the Warburg–Negelein values. To measure the rate of photosynthesis, Warburg and Negelein had chosen the first five minutes of a light period, which included a sudden and significant increase in pressure, which was not photosynthetic oxygen; while to measure the rate of respiration, which they used as their correction factor, Warburg and Negelein had chosen the first five minutes of a dark period, which comprised a significant decrease in pressure. Together, these time slots led to the efficiency of photosynthesis being greatly overestimated.

Emerson & Lewis (1941) demonstrated that the instability of γ was mainly due to dramatic changes in carbon dioxide pressure, while the oxygen pressure gave a relatively steady course of values:

> It is as if the cells contained some sort of reservoir which pours out carbon dioxide in the first minutes of illumination, and which must be filled again in the dark before the full respiration rate of carbon dioxide production can manifest itself.[22]

This phenomenon was shortly afterwards termed the "carbon dioxide burst".[23] Thus, Emerson and Lewis suggested that computing the rate of photosynthesis and its quantum yield from oxygen changes alone might take care of the problem. By this means, a maximum value of about 0.10 molecules of oxygen per absorbed quantum of light, under widely varying conditions and using no fewer than eleven different species of algae, was obtained. This value, equivalent to a minimum quantum requirement of

---

[22]Emerson & Lewis (1941), p. 794.

[23]Brown & Whittingham (1955) later showed, by mass spectroscopy, that it was indeed a release of carbon dioxide, not of molecular oxygen; in the recent literature, it has been related to "photorespiration".

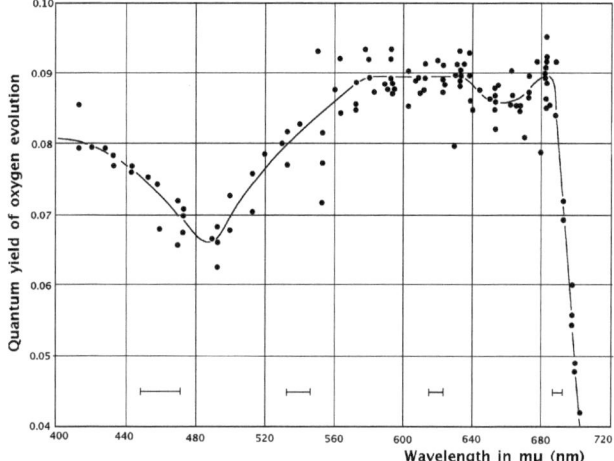

Figure II.7: The maximum quantum yield of photosynthesis at different wavelengths of light in the green alga *Chlorella*. Figure of Emerson and Lewis (1943), as redrawn by Govindjee & Björn (2011). Note that the minimum quantum requirement measured here was 11 ±1 light quanta per oxygen evolved, and that there was a sharp drop in the yield at ∼685 nm, called the "Red Drop". The dip around 490 nm is due to the inefficiency of carotenoids, which are the pigments absorbing light in this region.

10 per oxygen molecule, was in satisfactory agreement with the values reported by Magee et al. (1939), although the earlier group had arrived at it using very different methods. Emerson & Lewis (1941) were convinced that this was a fair approximation of the actual value, and considered the issue to be settled.

THE RED DROP (1943)

Emerson and Lewis then set out to investigate the maximum quantum yield of oxygen evolution in different wavelengths of light – and in doing so they hit upon a phenomenon that was to have lasting significance. It was the discovery of the "Red Drop" in photosynthetic efficiency: quantum efficiency of photosynthesis dropped sharply beyond 685 nm even though chlorophyll a was still absorbing light. (See Figure II.7 for the course of quantum yield of oxygen evolution at different wavelengths.)

The results were published in Emerson & Lewis (1943). The starting point was given by the observation that, given Einstein's Law of

Photochemical Equivalence, the efficiency of photosynthesis should be independent of the wavelength of light, at least for the range of the spectrum in which chlorophyll absorption occurs. (The underlying assumption was that the primary photochemical process was proportional only to the number of absorbed quanta, irrespective of their wavelength.) Warburg and Negelein's measurements of 1923 had been received up to then as demonstrating exactly this independence; however, since Emerson and Lewis considered that the work done by Warburg and Negelein was methodologically flawed, they saw a definite need for more precise information, *"particularly in the red region where chlorophyll* a *is the principal light-absorbing pigment"* (p. 165). To their surprise, they found the following:

> *In the course of the experimental work, two phenomena were encountered which raised special problems in the measurement of the quantum yield in certain portions of the spectrum. Exposure of cells to the blue-green region sometimes caused a considerable increase in the apparent rate of respiration. And an unexpectedly sharp decline in the quantum yield was observed in the far red.*[24]

Emerson and Lewis considered these two observations *"at least as significant as the original purposes of the work"* (p. 166), and hence discussed them at some length. The first of these findings again undermined one of the previously held fundamental methodical assumptions: up to this point all photosynthesis measurements, using manometry, had used the same respiration correction factor obtained in the dark for all conditions; now, Emerson & Lewis (1943) had found that the effect of light-induced oxygen consumption (whether this was respiration in the strict sense or not) could vary significantly at certain wavelengths of blue light, around 480 nm. Not all cells were equally sensitive to this wavelength region; however, the effect was always observed so that one had to be aware of the possibility of variation under different conditions, which might introduce yet another source of systematic error to the photosynthesis rates measured. For example, Emerson & Lewis (1943) reported that *"under the conditions of the quantum yield measurements, the rate of respiration tends to decline slowly over a period of several hours"* (pp. 169–170) , regardless of the kind of illumination or other parameters, while the rate of decline was not the same during continuous light or alternating light and dark periods. Notwithstanding these findings, the assumption that by using 10-minute intervals the rate of respiration in the dark led to a close estimate of its rate in the light, remained part of the body of standard knowledge for a surprisingly long time.

---

[24]Emerson & Lewis (1943), p. 166.

Second, Emerson and Lewis found that although the quantum yield was roughly constant in the region 580 to 685 nm, the yield dropped sharply beyond 685 nm, i.e., towards the infrared region of the spectrum. (See Figure II.7 for a graph of their data; the decline in the quantum yield in the blue-green region – a large dip was at around 490 nm – is due to the low efficiency of energy transfer from carotenoids to chlorophyll a.) All attempts to measure photosynthetic yield in the regions beyond 700 nm were unsuccessful. This was the phenomenon that later became known as the "Red Drop" of photosynthesis efficiency. The fact is that even at these higher wavelengths, that is, above 685 nm, chlorophyll a still absorbed light, and no pigments were known to compete with chlorophyll in this region. Emerson and Lewis were completely at a loss as to how to explain this finding. An explanation was only found many years later, in the second half of the 1950s, when it became clear that two photosystems were involved in photosynthesis.

4   THE PHOTOSYNTHESIS RESEARCHERS IN TIMES OF WAR

ROBERT EMERSON, C. STACY FRENCH AND WILLIAM ARNOLD

In December 1941, after the attack on the headquarters of the US Pacific Fleet at Pearl Harbor, Hawaii, the United States entered the Second World War, which was already in its third year in Europe. This profoundly changed most scientists' research agendas, including photosynthesis researchers in the United States, so that quantum yield studies and most other projects were put aside until after 1945. The researchers reacted in a variety of ways in order to cope with the new circumstances. Emerson, for example, had no desire to become involved in any war-related projects. Furthermore, he was thoroughly disgusted with how, from one day to the next, US citizens of Japanese origin were treated. Camps were erected in which these people, whom the authorities considered a threat to the national security, were interned and deprived of ways to meaningfully spend their time and make use of their abilities. Emerson used his local influence to launch a project to help alleviate this situation, at least in California. *"Our aim was to develop the desert shrub, guayule, as a source of rubber which could be produced under American living standards, without resort to the exploitation of native labor in Southeast Asia,"* Emerson later wrote in an autobiographical note.[25] To Emerson's great satisfaction, the project turned out to be a major success – not only in scientific terms, but also in terms of giving purpose

---

[25] Quoted in Rabinowitch (1961), p. 115.

Figure II.8: C. Stacy French (right, sitting) and one of his associates, Harold W. Milner (left, standing), at the Carnegie Institution of Washington in Stanford (ca. 1960). (Courtesy of the Department of Plant Biology Library, CIW, Stanford.)

to the lives of a number of deportees.[26] Emerson's closest collaborator in this project was M. Shimpe Nishimura, who skilfully combined the expertise of professional gardening with his previous studies of physics at the Caltech (both of which had been brutally interrupted upon his internment). Nishimura later became Emerson's assistant at Urbana, Illinois.

Not unlike Emerson, Charles Stacy French (1907–1995), a postdoctoral student of Emerson's at Harvard, who later became an important figure of photosynthesis research himself (and Director of the Plant Biology Department of the Carnegie Institution of Washington), registered himself as a "conscientious objector", yet he could only maintain this status by finding acceptable alternative occupations.[27] (See Figure II.8 for a photograph of French.) As French wrote in his autobiography: *"Draft dodging led me at various times into teaching elementary physics, researching chlorophyll-containing paint for camouflage purposes, and*

---

[26]For two of the resulting publications, see Nishimura, Emerson, Hata & Kageyama (1944) and Nishimura, Hirosawa & Emerson (1947).

[27]For biographical information on French, see e.g. Govindjee & Fork (2006).

Figure II.9: James Franck (left) and William Arnold (right). This picture was presumably taken in the 1950s in a restaurant, perhaps in the Mountain view hotel, when Oak Ridge National Laboratory (ORNL) had a conference in Gatlinburg, Tennessee. (Courtesy of Helen A. Herron, Arnold's daughter; date and location according to her memory.)

a long project on mold selection for penicillin production".[28] William Arnold's career took another turn. In 1941, he was made Assistant Professor of Biophysics at Stanford University. However, while Arnold was entertaining joyful visions of *"spending winters on the campus of Stanford, and summers at the Hopkins Marine Station,"* he received a letter from Princeton University, asking him *"to take part in an investigation of anti-aircraft fire"*, supported by the Office of Scientific Research and Development (OSRD), which he eventually accepted.[29]

JAMES FRANCK AND EUGENE RABINOWITCH

Rieke's former advisor, James Franck (1882–1964), had enjoyed happy years as a professor for Experimental Physics at the University of Göttingen, Germany, which abruptly ended after the Nazi Government came to power in 1933.[30] (See Figure II.9 for a photograph of Franck, together with Arnold.) Following the infamous "Law for the Restoration of the Professional Civil Service", issued on 7 April 1933, all persons with at least one Jewish grandparent were dismissed from the German civil ser-

---

[28]French (1979), p. 12.

[29]Arnold (1991), p. 77.

[30]For biographical information on Franck, see Beyerchen (1996), Rosenberg (2004) and Lemmerich (2007).

vice, which included university academics.[31] And although Franck, as a First World War veteran, would have fallen under the only exemption clause to this law, he publicly resigned from his professorship at Göttingen in protest. This courageous step caused an enormous stir, nationally and internationally, among scientists, politicians and the wider public. The consequences were far-reaching. Although Franck had originally intended to stay in Germany, he soon realized that he would be unable to find a new academic post or a position in industry in his home country as long as the political circumstances did not change. Thus, after a short stay at the Johns Hopkins University in Baltimore, USA, Franck spent a year at Niels Bohr's institute in Copenhagen, Denmark. In the meantime a professorship at Johns Hopkins had been arranged for him, which he was able to accept in 1935. It was during these first years of exile that Franck became interested in the photochemical aspects of photosynthesis. Starting in 1942, however, Franck took part in the research effort of the "Metallurgical Laboratory", set up at the University of Chicago to explore the possibilities of constructing an atomic bomb.[32]

Franck's assistant in Göttingen was Eugene Rabinowitch (1901–1973), also a Jew, who took a similar route – from Germany via Copenhagen and London – to the United States, although he found it much harder than Franck to obtain a new position.[33] (See Figure II.10 for a photograph of Rabinowitch, together with another renowned photosynthesis researcher, Louis N. M. Duysens.) Rabinowitch arrived in Copenhagen in 1934, where he spent six happy months; however, as more and more German refugees turned to Bohr for help, the possibilities for workspace and payment became restricted. Thus, in 1934 Rabinowitch went to continue his photochemical work in London, University College, as a research associate of the physical chemist Frederick G. Donnan (1870–1956). It was during these years that Rabinowitch became thoroughly interested in chlorophyll and its role in photosynthesis. At the same time Franck had also intensified his work on these topics, and the two of them stayed in regular correspondence. However, they wrote to each other not only on the topic of chlorophyll – rather, Rabinowitch hoped to follow Franck to the United States. But Franck was not yet in a position to help. In 1936, on March 2, Franck wrote to Rabinowitch:

---

[31]An English translation of the pertinent documents of the Nazi period, including the text of the "Law for the Restoration ...", as well as perceptive commentaries and useful background information, can be found in Hentschel (1996), pp. 21–34.

[32]See, e.g., Lemmerich (2007), pp. 243–251. For recent contributions on the history of the Manhattan project, see, e.g., Baggot (2010), Kelly (2007), Hughes (2003).

[33]For biographical information on Rabinowitch, see Bannister (1972), Govindjee (2004), A. Rabinowitch (2005).

Figure II.10: Eugene Rabinowitch (right) and the biophysicist and photosynthesis researcher Louis N. M. Duysens (left). (Photograph taken in the late 1960s by Govindjee at a conference on photosynthesis.)

I hope that the conditions will change, but at the moment there is not only the difficulty with the money available but also a sentiment against the absorption of too many foreigners. If there is at all a chance to find a place in England, you should take it, even if it is not good. I would ask you also to think over the question of going to Russia. I know how many sentiments you feel against it, but more and more the world becomes narrower and greyer. Think it over carefully.[34]

Eventually, Rabinowitch succeeded in going on a lecture trip to the United States. A happy consequence of this was that he was offered a position as a research associate at the Massachusetts Institute of Technology (MIT) under a grant from the Cabot industries, to work on the chemical utilization of light energy, where Rabinowitch then studied, most of his time, the so-called photogalvanic effect. Eventually, also Rabinowitch received an invitation to join the Metallurgical Laboratory, which, however, he only accepted in 1943 (because the necessary clearance would only be issued five years after having entered the United States). Rabinowitch arrived in Chicago just a few weeks after Enrico Fermi (1901–1954) had

---

[34]Franck to Rabinowitch on 2 March 1936. Franck, James. Papers, [Box 7, Folder 1], Special Collections Research Center, University of Chicago Library.

successfully established a self-sustaining nuclear chain reaction – that is, he came at exactly the time when everybody began to realize that building an atomic bomb really was a feasible project.

OTTO WARBURG

Otto Warburg's fortunes during the war were quite remarkable: he not only survived the Nazi period, he even remained, until 1945, in his original position, as the Director of the Kaiser Wilhelm Institute of Cell Physiology (founded in 1931 in Berlin-Dahlem). This was despite the fact that Warburg was considered a "half Jew" by the Nazis, even though Warburg's mother was of Protestant origin (so that, according to traditional Jewish law, Warburg was not a Jew at all) and his father had converted to Protestantism long before the birth of his son.[35] (In addition, Otto Warburg had always distanced himself explicitly from Judaism in general and from the Jewish part of his own family in particular). Warburg's treatment by the Nazis was exceptional, given the fact that so many other people of the same ancestry, regardless of their positions, were banished, deported or killed.[36] Warburg's fortune during the years of the Nazi regime has puzzled many historians. Particularly in the United States, many people suspected that Warburg collaborated to some extent with the Nazis.[37] Yet as far as is known today, no evidence for this assumption has come to the fore – if one does not include the lack of direct resistance as a form of collaboration. There is, on the other hand, ample evidence of the contempt Warburg felt for the new Government, which he largely tried to ignore. The special status of Warburg's institute, which was financed mostly by the Rockefeller Foundation, probably contributed to the fact that Warburg was, for a long time, exempted from the usual regulations within the Kaiser Wilhelm Society. Yet, in the end, Warburg most probably survived because of the continuous efforts of a number of influential friends in the fields of politics, economics and science, who repeatedly managed to get him out of difficult situations.[38]

---

[35] For biographical information on Warburg, see the references given on page 11.

[36] On the fate of other scientists in Warburg's discipline, see, e.g., Deichmann (2001a) and Deichmann (2001b).

[37] The plant physiologist Albert Frenkel recalled in an interview with Govindjee (on 8 Sept. 2007) that when Warburg was in the US in 1948/49, Gaffron had organised a party for him at Woods Hole, Massachusetts. It was at this party that a wife of one of the professors at Caltech bluntly asked Warburg why he had stayed in Germany *"when the Nazis were doing such bad things"*. To which Warburg replied: *"I wanted to protect my co-workers"*. He then added: *"What could I have done?"* Whereupon she replied: *"You could have committed suicide!"* This, understandably, shocked Warburg and many others there.

[38] On this question, see, in addition to the general biographical literature, Nickelsen (2009a) and Macrakis (1993), p. 64 and p. 226, footnote 53.

Warburg had few illusions about his prospects as a scientist of half-Jewish ancestry in a national-socialist Germany; yet, he repeatedly emphasised that he was determined not to be dispelled *"by a handful of arbitrary criminals"* and that he would continue to work – and so he did, for a surprisingly long time.[39] It was only after repeated bombing had damaged virtually all the laboratory's windows that Warburg's institute was evacuated, in the summer of 1943, to a manor in the environs of Berlin called Schloss Seehaus (located in the village of Liebenberg, in the district of Templin), which was completely refurbished for this purpose.

The Russian front arrived in Liebenberg in April 1945 and it was not long until the Red Army took over the village. During the course of the occupation, Warburg's institute in Schloss Seehaus was completely cleared out: all the instruments, chemicals, benches, furniture and glasswork were taken by the Red Army. And although later the Russian commander of the occupied zone, Marshal Zhukov, personally apologized for the plundering and commanded that everything be immediately returned, the instruments and the furniture were never seen again. Consequently, the Kaiser Wilhelm Society abandoned the building in Liebenberg, which was then taken over by the local hospital. In June 1945 the original building of Warburg's institute in Dahlem was also occupied, this time by the Allied High Command in Berlin. Thereupon, Warburg dismissed all his employees. This was the end of his renowned Kaiser Wilhelm Institute (which, of course, would after the war be re-established as part of the newly founded Max Planck Society). From a letter that Warburg wrote to his sister Lotte on 13 January 1946, it transpires that he had already started thinking about a way out of his situation:

> I am living in my house in Gary Street again [in the Dahlem quarter of Berlin] (American Sector), and thanks to the Americans and Russians I am neither starving nor freezing. Until the end of September I stayed with Jacob [Heiss], whom I saved, with much effort, from military service and the Volkssturm, and who is well, in Rügen. We were then brought to Dahlem in Russian cars, with all our belongings. Four weeks ago, Marshal Zhukov fetched the two horses from Rügen, and asked me, after I had eaten with him in Babelsberg, whether I had any other requests. Now, the horses are back in Düppel, and my private life has returned to normal.
>
> Less favorable is the situation concerning my scientific work. I cannot yet say what I am going to do; of course, I have received several offers. But you know, from 1933, that I am not a friend of emigration, as this means that one's quality of life, whatever happens, deteriorates considerably. For the moment, I am staying

---

[39] Rüskamp (1989), p. 252.

put – with an institute, if possible; if not, without an institute – and perhaps only go and work as a guest in other countries. As a guest – who will definitely, after a conceivable period of time, return to his home country – one is usually welcome. ([The saying] "fish and visitors stink after 3 days" is a bit exaggerated, if one not only eats and drinks in the host country but also does some work.)[40]

A complementary account of how Warburg was treated after the war can be taken from a most informative report written by the renowned chemist Roger Adams (1889–1971), who went to Berlin from November 1945 to February 1946, as Scientific Advisor to the Military Governor of Germany.[41] Adams confirmed that, after Warburg had been *"thoroughly robbed"* by the Russians, *"he had experienced marked kindness on the part of the Russian authorities"*:

> *The Russians were solicitous of his welfare and generous in their gifts of food and fuel. It was apparent, however, that they had no intention of permitting his departure from the island. His journey to Berlin, consequently, was undertaken without their approval.[42]*

The report further describes that after Warburg's arrival in Dahlem – then the American Sector of Berlin – his situation became rather difficult. Warburg was regularly called upon by Russian representatives, among those Marshal Zhukov himself, who apparently tried to entice him into the Russian sector of the city, or into the Soviet Union proper. Warburg not only received food and fuel and was given back his two horses; he even received a B.M.W. (*Bayerische Motoren Werke*) car as a gift from Zhukov, together with a letter confirming that the car was given to Warburg as his own property. Obviously, other Russians did not share Zhukov's attitude, as transpired one month later, in February 1946:

> *Dr. Warburg's secretary, while driving in Dr. Warburg's automobile, was intercepted by two Russian officers and an enlisted man, also driving an automobile, at Luetzow Platz in the British sector of the city. The Russians forcibly evicted the secretary from*

---

[40] Otto Warburg to Lotte, 13 January 1946; translation by one of the authors (KN). The originally German document is quoted in Werner (1991), pp. 355–356, doc. 128. Note that Warburg was very fond of both his horses and his dogs.

[41] Roger Adams Papers, 1812-1971, held in the University of Illinois Archives, Record Series 15/05/023, Box 58. University of Illinois Archives. The following quotes are all taken from this document. This 5-page report has so far escaped the notice of all biographers of Warburg. It is probable that Roger Adams got to know Warburg already before the First World War, when Adams was in Berlin to study with Emil Fischer, Otto Diels, and Richard Willstätter.

[42] Roger Adams Papers, 1812-1971, Record Series 15/05/023, Box 58. University of Illinois Archives. Quote from p. 1.

Dr. Warburg's automobile and tore up Marshal Zhukov's letter. In their unsuccessful attempt to rob the secretary several shots were fired by the Russians, but no one was killed or wounded. The next morning Russian authorities at Karlshorst were not helpful and suggested that the Russians in question were probably American soldiers dressed in Red Army uniforms.[43]

The problem at that time was that it was not entirely clear whether Warburg "belonged" to the Russian or the American sector: He was living both on the island of Rügen (Russian zone) and in Berlin-Dahlem (American zone); while the location of his institute was equally unclear: was it Liebenberg (Russian zone) or Dahlem (American zone)? Adams tried to help Warburg: the plan was to engage Warburg as a scientific consultant of FIAT, in the company's Berlin office. Adams's hope was that by this move *"some small measure of protection might be afforded him from inopportune Russian advances"* (p. 3). However, after a delay of a month and a half, the request to employ Warburg was refused, with reference to an interview with Warburg by Public Safety, Special Branch, carried out on 27 December 1945. A copy of the interview protocol has survived. First, Warburg's own perspective on the events in the Nazi period was given:

Subject stated that in 1933 he was informed by the Ministry of Culture that he should have no worries about his half-Jewish ancestry as far as his work and position was concerned. He attributed this to the fact that his work was supported by the Rockefeller Institute in New York. In 1938, he stated, he was told that he would not be permitted to attend an international scientific meeting in Switzerland. He went anyway, telling the superiors that he would quit his job if he was not given the necessary permits. Subject further stated that in 1941 he was told that he would have to resign his position. He went over the head of the Minister of Culture and was told to continue his cancer research in the personal interest of Hitler and through the personal intercession of Philip Bouhler, "Reichsleiter" of the NSDAP, "SS-Gruppenführer" and Chief of the Chancellery of the Fuehrer. Subject attributes this to Hitler's fear of cancer.[44]

Then, the interview went further to find out what Warburg thought about Germany's future. Warburg, apparently, was very blunt in his answer:

---

[43] Roger Adams Papers, 1812-1971, Record Series 15/05/023, Box 58. University of Illinois Archives. Quote from pp. 2-3.

[44] Roger Adams Papers, 1812-1971, Record Series 15/05/023, Box 58. University of Illinois Archives. Quote from p. 4.

> *Subject further stated that the German people are too stupid po-litically to achieve self-government on a democratic basis. It will take a very long time to change this situation, at least twenty years, and in the meantime Germany must have a government imposed by the Allies. Subject stated that he had never voted or belonged to any party because he considered all such activity a stupidity. Subject further stated that militarism is most natural for the Germans and admitted that he considered his own military service as a very pleasant time and a life of the soldier worthy and honourable, "provided the army in question was used in the interest of humanity and civilization".[45]*

This was sufficient for the interviewer to stop any possible employment of Warburg as a consultant:

> *This agent feels that the above interview is sufficient to establish the fact that Subject is completely unsuited for the position of Con-sultant to OMGUS [Office for Military Government for Germany (U.S.)].[46] He does not have the qualifications laid down by General Clay i.e. "known liberal, statesmanlike qualities and views" etc.[47]*

The report ended with a plea to help Warburg in spite of his lack of statesmanlike qualities: *"Throughout last fall, despite his considerable fear and dread, Dr. Warburg retained always his dignity and wry sense of humor. At present he is a very tired man primarily concerned with seeking some possibility of peace"* (p. 5). In view of the undeniable attempts from part of the Russians to win Warburg for their country, Adams added, the American authorities should take on responsibility for Warburg, who, after all, was resident in the American sector of Berlin, and secure *"some kind of protection for him from Russian advances"* (p. 5).

Warburg's personality was also a factor to consider for the Rock-efeller Foundation, which Warburg had turned to (via the American branch of the Warburg family) in order to find himself (together with two assistants) a position in the United States. However, the matter was not received favorably, although different persons gave different reasons, ranging from the suspicion that Warburg had collaborated with the Nazis

---

[45] Roger Adams Papers, 1812-1971, Record Series 15/05/023, Box 58. University of Illinois Archives. Quote from p. 4.

[46] The Office of Military Government, United States (OMGUS), based in Berlin, was the U.S. government established by the military in occupied Germany after the end of WW II. It was headed by General Lucius D. Clay and administered the American sectors of Germany in general and Berlin in particular. Its function was taken over, in December 1949, by the U.S. High Commissioner for Germany.

[47] Roger Adams Papers, 1812-1971, Record Series 15/05/023, Box 58. University of Illinois Archives. Quote from p. 4.

to the argument that Europe needed its scientists and, finally, to Warburg's well-known "prima donna-ness". Alan Gregg (1890–1957), then Director of the Medical Sciences Division of the Rockefeller Foundation, bluntly summarized his personal reason for not awarding any more grants to Warburg:

> My main reason would be that his life work is pretty largely done and what remains from now on would require a disproportionate amount of money and effort in any other country than Germany, and it cannot be done there, either.[48]

These then were the circumstances in which Warburg found himself at the beginning of 1946. Notwithstanding the insecurity of his position, Warburg, aware of his status in science, was nevertheless optimistic. It is admirable that, even during these hard years, he never gave up his scientific pursuits. Warburg had no satisfactory infrastructure at his disposal and, given the state of the country (Germany), there was hardly any hope that this situation was to change in the foreseeable future. Once the war was over, however, Warburg immediately began catching up with the international scientific literature. One of the first things that he published was a short note on the quantum requirement of photosynthesis, Warburg (1945), which he wrote in response to the papers by Emerson and Lewis (1939, 1941, 1943) and to a review of the subject written by Franck & Gaffron (1941), in which the authors announced that the issue had been settled in favor of a minimal quantum requirement of twelve. Franck and Gaffron wrote:

> We know now that the high quantum efficiency mentioned is only apparent, and that the true efficiency is only a third of it, namely, 12 quanta per CO_2 molecule reduced. The foundations on which the hypotheses concerning the amazing efficiency and the four-step mechanism rested have disappeared.[49]

It is hardly surprising that Warburg strongly contested this perspective, and responded by vigorously reconfirming his earlier findings.

5 SETTING UP THE PHOTOSYNTHESIS PROJECT AT URBANA

Soon after the end of the Second World War, Robert Emerson was approached by the University of Illinois to set up a research laboratory dedicated to photosynthesis studies on the Urbana campus. Emerson had

---

[48] Alan Gregg to Robert L. Lambert, 27 October 1945; quoted in Werner (1991), p. 361.

[49] Franck & Gaffron (1941). p. 200.

Figure II.11: Emerson (right, sitting) is looking at the manometers that are attached to the big water tank (the temperature bath), in which the Warburg vessels connected to the other end of the manometer were hanging. Rabinowitch (left, standing) is intently looking at the set-up. (Photograph taken around 1950 in Emerson's laboratory in Urbana. Courtesy, University of Illinois Archives, image 0000194.tif.)

been looking for an opportunity to leave Caltech for some time already, yet he only accepted the attractive offer from Illinois on the condition that the university also hire a physicist or a physical chemist with an interest in photosynthesis, so that the project could be properly guided in both respects – plant physiology and physical chemistry.[50] His request was granted and, in 1946 Emerson was appointed Research Professor of Botany as well as one of eventually two Directors of the newly founded "Photosynthesis Project". (See Figures II.11 and II.12 for photographs of the laboratory.)

Right from the start, Emerson had been interested in the physical chemist Eugene Rabinowitch, who was then at the University of Chicago studying uranium chemistry as part of the Manhattan Project's Metallurgical Laboratory, as a potential second director of Urbana's photosynthesis project. The first volume of Rabinowitch's seminal monograph on photosynthesis had just been published, as Rabinowitch (1945), which made

---

[50]Cf. Govindjee (2004), p. 181.

Figure II.12: Emerson is in the small culture room in his laboratory in Urbana, where *Chlorella* cells were grown in special flasks. A gas stream of a definite composition (CO_2 mixed with air) passed through the flasks. The large gas tank can be seen in the front left of the picture. Emerson is adjusting a knob that controls the rate of flow of the gas. (Photograph taken around 1950. Courtesy, University of Illinois Archives, image 0000194.tif.)

him a particularly eligible candidate for the position.[51] Emerson himself had not studied much physics and chemistry and greatly respected those who were competent in these fields. However, at the same time, Emerson was fully aware of the limited reliability of even the best biological data in quantitative terms, and it was extremely hard to persuade him that, within margins of error, even imperfect measurements could be used to construct more comprehensive models. Personally, Emerson would rule out data as "n.g." (no good) whenever he believed that they had not been obtained with the greatest attention to consistency and precision in procedure.[52] Hence, although Emerson thought that the Photosynthesis Project also required a more theoretically oriented person, it had to be one with sufficient sensitivity towards the specific problems of biology. Rabinowitch seemed to meet these criteria. On 23 October 1946, Emerson

---

[51]The second volume of this monograph was published in two parts, as Rabinowitch (1951) and Rabinowitch (1956).

[52]Cf. Rabinowitch (1961).

wrote to the Dean of the College of Liberal Arts & Sciences, and the Dean of the Graduate College, to request that Rabinowitch be appointed Co-Director of the Photosynthesis Project. Emerson explained his choice by describing the intended scope of the laboratory's work, which, he argued, needed Rabinowitch's skills to complement his own interests and knowledge:

> *If he [Rabinowitch] is appointed, it will be our plan to make a joint attack on the problem of energy absorption and conversion in the green plant. My share of the program will be the study of photosynthesis as it takes place in the intact cells of lower plants. Mr. Rabinowitch will work on artificial systems, built either from components extracted from plant parts or from non-living material, which give promise of simulating the unique energy-storing aspects of the natural process of photosynthesis.*[53]

Emerson's request was granted, and thus started what (according to Rabinowitch) Warburg would later mockingly describe as the "Emerson–Rabinowitch photosynthetic unit". The arrangement was to prove most satisfactory: the combination of the two Directors' talents, characters and approaches did indeed prove fruitful, and the Photosynthesis Project in Urbana was to develop into one of the most active research centers on the subject. (A plaque on the South East side of the Natural History Building at the University of Illinois at Urbana recognizes the accomplishments in the field of photosynthesis achieved at this place; see Figure II.13.)

---

[53] Emerson to Carmichael on 23 October 1946, Robert Emerson Papers, 1923-61, Record Series 15/4/28, Box 1, Folder: Botany Department. University of Illinois Archives.

Figure II.13: The plaque in Urbana recognizing the pioneering work of Robert Emerson and Eugene Rabinowitch. The photograph shows Rajni Govindjee (extreme left) and Govindjee (co-author of this book, extreme right), the last two PhD students of Emerson. Also shown in this photograph is Ben Clegg (2011 Emerson Scholarship Awardee), standing next to Rajni, and R.J. Cody Markelz (2011 Govindjee & R. Govindjee Awardee for Excellence in Biological Sciences). Ben is wearing Emerson's apron and holding Emerson's hand spectroscope, whereas Cody is wearing the glasses Emerson wore when he did glassblowing. (Photograph taken in 2011 by Martha Plummer.)

Chapter III

THE CONTROVERSY DEVELOPS

1 WARBURG COMES TO THE UNITED STATES

On 28 November 1947, Emerson wrote his first letter to Warburg since losing touch with him after 1939.[1] Therein, Emerson reported how he had heard, through Roger Adams, that Warburg had responded to the challenge of the Warburg–Negelein quantum yield values posed by Emerson and Lewis (1939, 1941, 1943). Emerson informed Warburg that he finally had been able to obtain the German paper, Warburg (1945); and that he had translated it into English. This translation was published as Warburg (1948) in the American Journal of Botany; therein, Warburg described the papers from the Madison group, published in 1938 and 1939, as being methodically flawed and the critique by Emerson and Lewis as being insubstantial.[2] At the same time, Warburg fully confirmed the quantum requirement values of 1923, based on new measurements that he had taken using the two-vessel method.

With hindsight one can already find in this first response of Warburg some of the leitmotifs of the ensuing controversy: for example, Warburg's arrogant contempt of Emerson's findings. After all, one could read between the lines, Warburg was the master who had developed the methods, which Emerson had only learned from him much later as Warburg's student. In fact, Warburg (1948) wrote that he *"would be astonished if Emerson had found the truth with our methods while we ourselves had fallen into error in our application of the same method"* (p. 194). Warburg continued to explain why he considered Emerson's approach to be flawed:

> *The disadvantage of this method [of Emerson's] is that the bicarbonate solutions are unphysiological from the standpoint of their chemical composition, osmotic pressure, and pH. The hydrogen ion concentration of the least alkaline bicarbonate solution is 10.0–9.4 and thus differs from the physiological hydrogen ion concentration for Chlorella by more than four orders of magnitude. [...] It would never have occurred to us to measure the most delicate*

---

[1] Archive of the Berlin-Brandenburg Academy of Sciences and Humanities, Berlin, Germany (BBAW); NL Warburg 262; Emerson to Warburg on 28 November 1947.

[2] Note that in August of the same year, 1948, Eugene Rabinowitch published a review of the state of the art in photosynthesis research for the Scientific American; see Rabinowitch (1948). Therein, he described the question of the maximum quantum yield as *"still unsettled"*, while *"the weight of the evidence favors the higher value"* (p. 30).

of all biochemical processes, the conversion of light energy into chemical energy, in a medium in which the very survival of the cells seems remarkable. Not so Emerson. He reasons, correctly, that by determining the yield in bicarbonate solution all his concern about the assimilatory quotient is eliminated. He makes the unjustifiable assumption, however, that the effect of the unphysiological medium can be neglected for the sake of this methodological simplification.[3]

Warburg wrote that, in his own experiments, he had found that the assimilatory quotient γ was -0.93, which was sufficiently close to -1, even for intervals of only five minutes. Thus, Warburg held that *"through this result Emerson's main objection to our yield determination has been refuted: the physically and physiologically improbable allegation that the photochemical reduction of carbon dioxide is introduced by an outburst of carbon dioxide"* (p. 195). Likewise, Warburg (1948) dismissed Emerson's second objection – that the pressure changes in the first minutes of illumination were drastically different from the remaining period: *"With our new method, the method of manometric γ determination, we found nothing of the sort. With our old method, which Emerson used, we sometimes, particularly at rather high light intensities, observed small 'Emerson' effects, which quite likely originated from nothing other than bubble formation"* (p. 195). In these cases, Warburg reported, he had rejected the readings taken at the beginning of a light or dark period and only used the readings taken towards the end of the respective period. As in 1923, he still found *"a quantum requirement of 4 to 5 per molecule of evolved oxygen"* (p. 195). In these passages, the second leitmotif of the controversy emerged: Warburg's habit of not answering objections head on, but rather of presenting new data that he had obtained by altering his methods – so that the critic then needed to demonstrate, first of all, whether the earlier objections also held true for the new set-up. However, at this early stage of the controversy, Emerson chose not to pick on these by-passes of Warburg's; instead he made the following suggestion in a letter to Warburg of 1947:

> *It is now being discussed in America how to explain the incon-sistency in determining the yield of assimilation. It seems to us that it would be best if we could observe the same phenomena in a laboratory together and calculate the yield in the same manner. If Germany had not been so badly damaged and if you still had your laboratory, I would suggest that I come to visit you in Berlin. But as far as I have heard, at the moment it is impossible for you to undertake any kind of scientific work. Hence, I suggest that you*

---

[3]Warburg (1948), p. 194.

visit us here and carry out some comparative experiments in our laboratory. We are still far from being as well equipped as you were in Dahlem, but nevertheless our laboratory is sufficiently equipped for carrying out quantum yield measurements. You may want to bring [Fritz] Kubowitz with you and your strain of algae, a Hefner lamp and whatever other instruments need to be compared.[4]

The University of Illinois's administration had already agreed to provide the necessary financial support, and Emerson suggested that this should be used to cover Warburg's and his laboratory assistant's traveling expenses as well as a salary for the two of them for six months (Warburg's assistant was assumed to be his long-standing collaborator Fritz Kubowitz.). Emerson also announced that he would now apply for immigration permits from the US State Department, so that they would be ready in time.

Warburg answered on 19 December, 1947. He thanked Emerson for the invitation and said that he would come with Wilhelm Lüttgens as his assistant. (Emerson, of course, did not know that in 1944 Kubowitz had denounced Warburg to the Nazi authorities; Warburg had been saved thanks to some influential friends, and would never speak to Kubowitz again. Lüttgens was the only one among his long-standing collaborators whom Warburg still fully trusted.[5]) Warburg also wanted to bring his valet and secretary Jacob Heiss (1899–1984) with him. He would pay Heiss out of his own salary, and if necessary would also cover Heiss's traveling expenses – however, Warburg still needed a personal invitation for Heiss, otherwise it would be impossible for the latter to travel: at the time, German citizens were still not free to travel abroad. And to enter the United States, they also had to prove that they were politically unstained.

During the course of the following months, Warburg repeatedly changed his choice of assistant, his means of transport, payment and other details – all to Emerson's exasperation, since any one of these changes meant that he had to resume negotiations with both the university and immigration officials. In the end, Warburg brought only Heiss with him, and the two of them arrived by plane. Warburg was probably never aware of all the trouble Emerson went through in order to organize his visit. Emerson succinctly described his feelings in a letter to Hans Gaffron on 29 May 1948:

---

[4] Archive of the BBAW, NL Warburg 262. Emerson to Warburg on 28 November 1947. Original letter in German; translation by one of the authors (KN).

[5] For background information on this episode, see, e.g., Nickelsen (2008a).

Dear Hans:

When I saw a letter from you in yesterday's mail, I hoped it would say you planned to come down and visit us over Memorial Day week-end. The weather is perfect today, and I feel it is high time you saw our laboratory. Maybe you will come while Warburg is here. It really looks as if he would come, there is mail here for him, from Paris.

[Carl] Cori [the physiologist] is right, his [Warburg's] visit is sure to lead to a lot of grief. In fact, just trying to arrange for the visit has kept me busy for a large part of the winter. After all our efforts to provide Warburg with an assistant of his own choosing, it turns out the man (Gustav Ernst Lau) cannot come because he lives in the Russian zone. Seems to me Warburg might have thought through of this difficulty a few months ago, instead of now, when he is about ready to leave. Last report I had was that he and Heiss might leave by June 1st. I hear they have 400 kilos of baggage and a poodle, on all of which they expect the Univ. of Illinois to pay transportation. It will turn out that the reason Warburg wants to leave Germany is because the American administration has been unable to get any more of that good German dog-food, made of pure beef-steak, the only thing the poodle will eat. There will be Hell to pay when he finds that in America they feed horse-meat to dogs! And imagine the problem of finding housing for Warburg, Heiss, and a poodle!

Yes, I believe Cori is right, but I hope it will be worth the trouble, to get this matter settled. Bob.[6]

No mention was ever made of the poodle again, so it can be assumed that it remained in Germany. Warburg, though, entered the United States, together with Heiss and an enormous amount of luggage, on 26 June 1948. He left a disastrous first impression on Emerson and others, as one learns from a description recorded in an interview with the German chemist Karl Friedrich Bonhoeffer (1899–1957):

Otto Warburg was traveling with [a] diener [servant] and five or six large crates of personal belongings. He was going to the University of Illinois, presumably on a permanent appointment. He was met, several hours after the arrival of the plane, by Professor Emerson. [...] Fellow travelers were either elderly German women clothed in their best black dresses and going to homes of sons or grandchildren in the United States, or young German brides of American GIs. Since the plane was over twelve hours late, practically none of these

---

[6]This letter is in private hands; thanks to the intercession of one of us (Govindjee), Peter Homann kindly made it available to the authors.

inexperienced travelers were met at the airport and each had their own problem: No knowledge of English, no American money, no ticket for air travel to Spokane, etc. W.[arburg] seemed completely selfish, being much more concerned with the probably undeclared gold nuggets in his baggage than with the problems of his fellow travelers. He was visibly annoyed by the fact that there were no airline officials before 7:00 A.M. to handle his possessions shipped as cargo.[7]

As Emerson was soon to experience, Warburg was never to make up for the bad impression he had made upon his arrival.

2   THE TIME SPENT AT URBANA

When Warburg arrived at Urbana, he immediately turned the laboratory upside down. Rabinowitch (1961) provides a lively description of how Warburg was accustomed to working in a laboratory that completely and utterly fulfilled his wishes; and, since Emerson's laboratory was not large enough for Warburg to have been given full command of a section, he and Emerson had to tolerate each other in the laboratory's communal areas. This was bound not to work smoothly. To his former colleague and friend Charlton M. Lewis, Emerson wrote on 8 October 1948, that he had found no time to look at Lewis's latest data: *"This is because of the pressure we are under to provide for Warburg, who has a way of setting the entire laboratory on its head almost every day."* Emerson found nothing to report himself, yet he added: *"I'm hoping there will be some progress with experiments before long."*[8] In the same vein, Emerson apologized also to others that he had neglected correspondence and potential obligations.[9]

Still, at least in the beginning of Warburg's stay, Emerson tried hard to make Warburg's stay as comfortable as possible. He had, for example, furnished Warburg with a personal assistant: Victor Schocken, who had only just come to Urbana from Berkeley and was originally destined to work for Rabinowitch. Instead, Emerson arranged that Schocken assisted Warburg in his work – Schocken was the only one among potential assistants who spoke German and Warburg refused to communicate in

---

[7]Quoted in Werner (1991), p. 382, doc. 147. Shelf mark of the original document: Archives of the Rockefeller Foundation, r.g.1.1., s.717, b.2, f.11. The story that Warburg had tried to sneak out some valuable items in order to sell them for dollars was also circulated by Hans Krebs.

[8]Emerson to Lewis on 8 Oct. 1948, Robert Emerson Papers, 1923-61, Record Series 15/4/28, Box 1, Folder: Lewis, Charlton. University of Illinois Archives.

[9]See for only one more example: Emerson to E. G. Pringsheim on 5 Nov. 1948, Robert Emerson Papers, 1923-61, Record Series 15/4/28, Box 1, Folder: Pringsheim, E.G. University of Illinois Archives.

Figure III.1: Warburg in the laboratory of Emerson in Urbana. The photograph appeared on the cover of the journal *Science* of July 30, 1948 (Vol. 108, issue 2796). In the same issue, Warburg's visit to the University of Illinois was announced (p. 101).

any other language. Furthermore, Emerson repeatedly made attempts to pave the path for Warburg to find a faculty position in the United States. The chemist Martin D. Kamen (1913–2002), co-discoverer of carbon-14, remembered in his autobiography that Emerson made arrangements to introduce Warburg to all workers in the field of photosynthesis who were able to come to Urbana, so that Warburg's search for a suitable position in the United States became widely known.[10] (Note that Warburg even made it to the cover page of the renowned journal *Science*; see Figure III.1). Yet, if all – or even most – of these encounters went like the meeting with Kamen, it is no surprise that nothing came of it. Emerson introduced Kamen to Warburg as a physicist – to Kamen's great surprise, since he had worked as a chemist, or rather biochemist, for the best of his life. The explanation given to him was the following:

> *Emerson explained later that had he identified me as a biochemist, I would have been dismissed curtly after a brief exchange of pleasantries. [...] [Warburg] was sharp and perceptive in his comments about current research, but exuded intellectual arrogance based on his awareness of the superior position he held among contemporary biochemists.*[11]

This might also have been the reason why Warburg constantly refused to give any lectures in Urbana – despite his explicit consent to do so when Emerson had asked him in advance. (This had been one of the conditions for having Warburg's stay financed by the University of Illinois.) Emerson wrote to Kamen on September 30, 1948: *"Warburg has resisted all efforts of Deans and Professors of Chemistry to persuade him to give bona fide lectures, but he has agreed to comment on other people's lectures."* Emerson continued, exasperated yet with a spark of hope: *"I can never foresee what his next impossible demand is going to be. But he is beginning to recognize that Emerson and Lewis found something funny about the method of Warburg and Negelein for measuring quantum yields. He does not accept our interpretation, but that may come later."*[12]

However, despite all this, Emerson still had high expectations that the visit would pay off. He truly believed that Warburg had come to carry out experiments with him and discuss the discrepancy between their results; yet nothing of the sort happened. Warburg proceeded to work in his own usual way and was not at all interested in Emerson or his work. The only positive reaction to Emerson's challenge that Warburg showed at Urbana was the fact that he had refined his new two-vessel technique

---

[10] Cf. Kamen (1985).

[11] Kamen (1985), p. 100.

[12] Quoted in Kamen (1985), p. 304.

for measuring quantum yield of photosynthesis. However, instead of discussing these or other details of the technique with Emerson, Warburg spent most of his time constructing an actinometer: a device to measure radiation intensity by way of monitoring a chemical reaction (in this case, the uptake of oxygen produced during the chlorophyllide reaction by thiourea). This was surprising, given the fact that Warburg had up to then used bolometers, which were far more accurate. In his paper of 1948, Warburg wrote that he had decided to abandon the experimental procedure of 1923, *"because of the danger of frothing"* (which he thought was the reason for the alleged carbon dioxide burst), and *"because it is unnecessarily cumbersome"*. Instead, Warburg suggested that light intensities should be measured by means of his chemical actinometer, which he considered *"so simple that it can be used as a laboratory experiment in a physiology course"*.[13] Although this was certainly true, one still wonders why he resorted to trading precision of measurement for ease of handling – there were certainly other ways of meeting Emerson's critique that Warburg's use of the bolometer needed to be improved (if this was indeed the motivation behind the changes Warburg made to his experimental procedure).

A dramatic turn of events finally occurred towards the end of the year. It is reasonable to assume that Emerson had gradually lost his patience with Warburg, and so had decided to try another way of getting Warburg to discuss quantum yields with him. In a letter to C. Stacy French, who wanted to meet Warburg at Urbana between 17 and 18 December, 1948, Emerson wrote:

> It so happens that we are having a number of guests that night, for a seminar discussion on quantum yields in photosynthesis, to be led by [the photochemist] Farrington Daniels at 9 o'clock Saturday morning, the 18th. There will also be a luncheon at noon Saturday, for as many of the photosynthesis people as can stay for it. I hope you will come to both the seminar and luncheon. We expect to have Rieke, Kamen, Commoner, Daniels, Stauffer, and probably some others. It is very fortunate that the date of your visit coincides with this meeting. Please let me know on what train you arrive, I'll probably be able to meet you.[14]

As can be taken from an earlier letter that Emerson had written to Kamen on 26 November, 1948, it had been agreed that Farrington Daniels, from Madison, would bring down some pieces of his apparatus to Urbana for Warburg to take a look at and make comments. Emerson

---

[13] Warburg (1948), pp. 208–209.

[14] Emerson to French on 3 Dec. 1948, Robert Emerson Papers, 1923-61, Record Series 15/4/28, Box 1, Folder: French, C. Stacy. University of Illinois Archives.

Figure III.2: Otto Warburg (right, writing in his notebook) and Dean Burk (left, standing and looking at what Warburg was writing); in the background are the manometers. (Photograph taken in Warburg's laboratory in Berlin, in the early 1950s. Reproduced from Krebs 1979, Figure 12; also published in Höxtermann 2007, Figure 10.)

wrote: *"Also, Warburg has proposed a procedure for measuring quantum yields upon which both of us can agree, and I am reasonably certain the results will leave him holding the bag".*[15] Emerson was clearly in a hurry to invite everybody who might be interested (and be valuable for the discussion), and the meeting, which was chaired by Daniels, unexpectedly developed into a large conference, with an audience of about a hundred, and with several speakers, besides Warburg, scheduled to give presentations.[16] Also present was Albert Frenkel (born in 1919), who had been an assistant to Emerson at Caltech, where the two of them became good friends (and who discovered later photophosphorylation in 'chromatophores' of anoxygenic photosynthetic bacteria); according to

---

[15]Quoted in Kamen (1985), p. 304.

[16]According to the News Gazette of 25 December, 1948, among the more renowned participants were Farrington Daniels, J. F. Stauffer, Foster Rieke, Barry Commoner, Martin Kamen, C. Stacy French, Allan H. Brown and Hans Gaffron. A note on this meeting, based on information provided by Tippo, was also published in *Science*, Vol. 109, on January 7, 1949, p. 25.

Frenkel, the meeting was civilized, and without the nasty quality that the controversy would later acquire – yet, nothing came out of it.[17]

The last chance to arrive at some sort of agreement came the day after Christmas 1948, about four weeks before Warburg intended to leave Urbana. Warburg had finally agreed to carry out some experiments alongside Emerson and his co-workers, and have the results judged by impartial observers. The two observers were the biochemist Dean Burk, who was then at the National Cancer Institute (NCI) in Bethesda, Maryland, and a colleague of his, John Z. Hearon, who had recently completed his PhD in biochemistry at the University of Minnesota. (See Figure III.2 for a photograph of Burk.) It was probably the botanist Oswald Tippo (1911–1999), at the time Head of the University of Illinois's Botany Department on the Urbana campus, who invited these two men to carry out this function. However, still no agreement was reached during this twelve-day period of common experimentation (26 December, 1948 to 6 January, 1949; note that the meeting was documented in the local newspaper, see Figure III.3). Warburg gave his side of the story in a letter he wrote to the plant physiologist Frederick C. Steward (1904–1993) of the University of Rochester (New York State), on 2 January 1949:

> *A few days ago I got cells to measure the yield in this way [i.e. by means of a recently developed actinometer] and I found, in the presence of two impartial observers, 4 quanta per molecule oxygen. Proceeding in exact [sic] the same way the next day two assistants of Dr. Emerson found for a different culture about 20 quanta per molecule of oxygen. So I came to the conclusion that the Chlorella cultures of Dr. Emerson are not suitable or at least unequal and I declared here that I could continue the experiments only if I had the control over the cultures of the Chlorella. This is a long story.*[18]

---

[17]Cf. Frenkel and Govindjee (personal communication [telephone interview], 8 September 2007. See also Frenkel (1993) for an autobiographical account of Warburg and how the quantum controversy came to the Marine Biological Laboratory at Woods Hole, Massachusetts, in 1949. Note, however, that Howard Gest, who is now Professor Emeritus at Indiana University, USA, and who had also attended this meeting remembers it differently: "I clearly remember Warburg's opening remarks, translated by Victor Schocken as he spoke. Warburg said that the crux of the disagreement was that American scientists simply did not know how to measure light intensity accurately, whereas he (Warburg) knew how because his famous father, Emil Warburg, taught him. Farrington Daniels immediately challenged this insult in a gentlemanly fashion. Warburg's arrogance was a key factor in prolonging an extraordinary expenditure of effort and research funds by a large number of dedicated scientists. Eventually there was a general consensus that Emerson was right and Warburg wrong about the maximum efficiency of photosynthesis in Chlorella." Personal communication (email) to Govindjee, 19 July 2011.

[18]Letter quoted in Walker (1992), with kind permission of Geoffrey Hind.

Figure III.3: Report on the experiments of Warburg and Emerson in the local Urbana newspaper, the Champaign–Urbana Courier, of 3 January 1949. Warburg is holding the differential manometer in his hand that everyone is looking at. Left to right: Victor Schocken, Shimpe Nishimura (sitting), Dean Burk (pointing to the manometer vessel), Oswald Tippo (looking over Warburg's shoulder), Otto Warburg (holding the manometer) and Robert Emerson (behind Warburg).

Warburg went on to explain that the question could only be settled if he found another place to stay for the rest of his time in the United States and inquired whether Steward would be able and willing to host him. In the end, Warburg joined Burk at the National Cancer Institute (NCI) in Bethesda; but before Warburg left Urbana, an official protocol, set up on 7 January 1949 and signed by all parties, documented the outcome of Warburg's stay in Urbana:

ON THE QUANTUM REQUIREMENT OF PHOTOSYNTHESIS

[...] *A simple manometric procedure, involving the photo-oxidation of thiourea sensitized by ethylchlorophyllide, has been developed and employed [to measure the light energy]. A new modification of the two-vessel method for determining oxygen and carbon dioxide exchange independently and simultaneously has been developed and employed [for photosynthesis measurements].*

With this method the photochemical evolution of carbon dioxide in certain cultures of green alga – Chlorella pyrenoidosa – has been repeatedly observed. In instances the ratio of carbon dioxide produced in light to oxygen produced in light has been as high as plus 4 instead of minus 1. From this it follows that the photochemical evolution of carbon dioxide could invalidate measurements of the efficiency of photosynthesis if it is not taken into account. [This paragraph was confirmed by Warburg's signature]

Our recent measurements by the new methods have given quantum requirements for oxygen production, which vary from 4-6 as a minimum to virtually infinity (no yield), apparently depending upon cell conditions. [This paragraph was confirmed by Emerson's signature.][19]

Thus, in the end both parties acknowledged that under some conditions the data purported by the opponent were in fact obtained; yet no agreement was reached about how significant these data were and how they should be interpreted. Burk suggested that the text be used as the basis of a jointly authored note of the opponents and the impartial observers that would be submitted to the journal Nature with the intention of informing the scientific public about the outcome of Warburg's visit to Urbana. However, on 10 January, 1949, Emerson cabled Burk to withhold publication (or omit Emerson's name) until further changes to the text had been agreed upon.[20] In a letter to Burk on 21 January 1949, Emerson explained his objections in more detail. First of all, he wrote,

---

[19]Quoted also in Werner (1991), p. 385, doc. 149. Original shelf mark: Archive of the BBAW, NL Warburg 265.

[20]Archive of the BBAW, NL Warburg 174. Emerson to Burk, 10 Jan. 1949.

the note, as it was, left readers with the impression that it covered the entire period of Warburg's stay in Urbana: *"It could be concluded that over the entire six-month period of Warburg's visit, we were never able to obtain consistent values for the quantum requirement. This implies a more serious criticism of conditions in my laboratory than is justified by the facts."* Emerson, therefore, insisted that they include the fact that *"the photosynthesis measurements referred to were all made during the 12 days of your [Burk's] visit"*.[21] Emerson mentioned to Burk that he had tried to amend the text by making minor insertions, yet ended up completely rewriting large portions of it.

Emerson had already shown the rewritten text to Warburg, who had flatly rejected it; nevertheless, Emerson felt that Burk should also see what he himself believed was a fair statement of the facts. Yet Emerson also added: *"The more I think about the problem, the less I feel that any useful purpose would be served by publication at the present time. The only cogent reason for a published statement is the one given by Dean [Louis N.] Ridenour [then, Dean of the Graduate College at Urbana] that it would reduce the circulation of unfounded rumors. In spite of the importance of this, I think it is outweighed by the fact that the data constitute a rather insufficient basis for the establishment of conclusions so important as those we are trying to reach. Any conclusions we draw now are subject to modification by the next few months of experimental work. This being so, I believe publication now is worse than no publication at all."*[22] The following two paragraphs are those rewritten sections of the original text:

> *New measurements of the quantum requirement of photosynthesis have been initiated, using the modified technique to avoid errors from possible photochemical evolution of carbon dioxide. Unfortunately, only two weeks were available for these experiments. It was during this period that Drs. Dean Burk and John Hearon were members of the group. The cultures available at this time showed widely divergent results, not only from one experiment to another, but also within most of the individual series of observations.* [Commentary in the margin to this last sentence: "This is absolutely untrue. Warburg"] *In certain experiments several successive 10-minute light exposures gave quantum requirements of 4 to 6, both per molecule of oxygen produced and per molecule of carbon dioxide consumed. But these exposures were proceeded or followed by others in which much larger numbers were obtained, running in some instances to infinity (no photosynthesis at all).* [Commentary in the margin "Not true. Warburg"]

---

[21] Archive of the BBAW, NL Warburg 174. Emerson to Burk, 21 Jan. 1949.
[22] Archive of the BBAW, NL Warburg 174. Emerson to Burk, 21 Jan. 1949.

These experiments raise again the possibility that the maximum efficiency of photosynthesis may be greater than the value (represented by about 10 absorbed quanta per molecule of evolved oxygen) that has become widely accepted among American investigators of the problem. However, an unambiguous and convincing determination of the maximum quantum yield of photosynthesis will require establishment of conditions leading to consistent and reproducible results. At present we are unable to offer a satisfactory explanation for the wide variability of the results reported here. The presence of appreciable bacterial contamination in all the Chlorella cultures used for these experiments raises the question to what extent processes other than photosynthesis may have contributed to the pressure changes attributed to illumination.[23]

Burk did not at all like the specification that the note was the result of two weeks – or rather: twelve days – of working together (he would have preferred to write that they all had worked together *"for several weeks"*, since, Burk hastened to add in his response to Emerson, he and Hearon had spent at least two weeks each on the problem before they arrived); nor did he agree with the last two sentences, which *"did not seem to me to be particularly true"*, as Burk stated. He closed his letter to Emerson with: *"I gather [...] that you are not keen on publishing jointly at present, and would prefer the various parties concerned to go their own way separately, presumably after further work."*[24]

Thus, even after Warburg had spent six months in Urbana, no resolution of the controversy between Warburg and Emerson seemed to be in sight: Warburg's 4 to 5 quanta per oxygen molecule stood against Emerson's value of 8 to 12 quanta (which was in agreement with the measurements that Rieke, Arnold and Magee et al. had made; see Chapter II). While Emerson later spoke of being thoroughly depressed at the outcome, Warburg announced his victory to everybody who would listen. *"It was as [if] somebody put it [sic] here a drama watched by all America and the happy end was the victory of truth,"* Warburg wrote to Tippo, after having left Urbana.[25] Warburg also used every possible opportunity to belittle Emerson and his work. For example, on 21 January 1949 Warburg wrote to C. Stacy French, after the latter had inquired whether Warburg would not like to stay a little longer in the United States:

---

[23] Archives of the Max Planck Society (MPG Archiv); III. Abt., Rep. 1, Nr. 187. Enclosed in a letter from Burk to Emerson on 25 January 1949.

[24] MPG Archiv; III. Abt., Rep. 1, Nr. 187. Burk to Emerson on 25 January 1949.

[25] Warburg, Otto to Tippo, Oswald, 17 Feb. 1949, Personal file of O. Tippo, (former) Botany Department, University of Illinois at Urbana, now: Department of Plant Biology.

> *Certainly I have not told [said] that it is impossible to work sci-*
> *entifically in the US. But I have told [said] that it is impossible in*
> *Emerson's laboratory. It seems to me that many scientists in this*
> *country are aware of this; but unfortunately nobody warned me. It*
> *is no crime to make mistakes in science. But it is another thing to*
> *fight established truth for years and years strewing sand into the*
> *mills of science.*[26]

In February, Warburg moved on to the NCI in Bethesda, where Burk had succeeded in securing him a six-month position (supported by the Public Health Service). He took Victor Schocken with him, who apparently had decided to swap parties in the controversy.

Warburg never forgave Emerson for insisting on his point. Even more, Warburg increasingly cast himself as the victim of a conspiracy of some American researchers – the "Midwest Gang", as Warburg would later call them. Besides Emerson and his colleagues and co-workers at Urbana, such as Rabinowitch, this "gang" also included Gaffron, Franck and Daniels. Andrew A. Benson, co-discoverer of the carbon reduction cycle in photosynthesis, recalled the following episode from an encounter with Warburg in 1952: *"On a beautiful afternoon I drove him [Warburg] and Herman Kalckar to 'Hamlet's castle' at Helsingør. Warburg peered through an iron gate into the darkness below, 'Ach, it's a perfect place for that Midwest Gang'."*[27] And although Warburg was known for his sharp tongue, keen sense of humor and even self-mockery (which he unfortunately lost in his later years), he might not have been entirely joking when he made this quip.

3   The "Re-Discovery" of High Efficiencies

Bethesda and Woods Hole

After four months at the NCI in Bethesda, Warburg, accompanied by Burk and Schocken, moved in June 1949 to the Marine Biological Station in Woods Hole, Massachusetts, where he would spend the last month of his stay in the USA. For this purpose, the whole experimental set-up for measuring photosynthetic quantum yields, including the culture vessels, Warburg apparatus etc., was transferred for the summer from Bethesda to Woods Hole. Warburg's appearance there greatly impressed those students that had come for summer courses, so that some still remember these weeks. The plant physiologist Miriam Jacob, for example, remembers the following:

---

[26]MPG Archiv; III. Abt., Rep. 1, Nr. 198. Warburg to French, 21 Jan. 1949.
[27]Benson (2002*b*); quoted also in Govindjee 2004, p. 184.

> *I was a student in the physiology course when it was announced that Professor Warburg would be joining the class and we would be using Warburg manometers to study the production of oxygen during photosynthesis. There were about 12 students and one sink to wash the glassware used by all. The next morning the sink was divided in two by a wooden partition and a sign was appended: This half of the sink is for Warburg's Warburgs.*[28]

It was in this physiology class that Warburg first had students try his new methods for quantum yield measurements, including the actinometer. Jacob remembers that Warburg held a lecture to explain his theory to the students:

> *Because he felt that his mastery of English was limited, he asked Victor Schocken (who came to Woods Hole with Dr. Warburg and was fluent in German) to present his material. During his presentation, Victor said: "Dr. Warburg believes that the number of quanta required is four". At this point Warburg leaped to his feet and said: "Vot do you mean, I believe? I know". The rest is history.*

Warburg even joined an excursion of the Physiology class, including a common picnic. Mauzerell remembered further how *"Warburg sat under a tree, eating lobster, attended by his valet, and holding forth to the attentive students who surrounded him"*. This scenery is also remembered by the plant physiologist Burlyn Michel, another participant in that particular physiology class – and one of those students, whose collaboration Warburg and Burk later would acknowledge in a paper published in 1950 – although Michel himself remembered, that he was not very impressed by these experiments, *"because of the small changes in manometer readings"*.[29] (See Figure III.4 for a photograph of Warburg at the picnic.)

In Woods Hole another confrontation with Emerson arose during the annual meeting of the Society for General Physiology, at which Emerson and Warburg met again to discuss maximum quantum yield of photosynthesis. This time the opponents became more outspoken and emotional; Michel recalled how surprised he was by the *"heated exchange between Emerson and Warburg following a presentation by Emerson, in which he disputed Warburg's claim of high efficiency"*. Again Emerson was thoroughly disappointed by the outcome of the meeting. Gaffron, who was in the audience, reported the course of events to the chemist and photosynthesis expert Martin Kamen:

---

[28]This and the following quote: Miriam Jacob (Mauzerall) to Govindjee; personal communication [email], 9 December 2007.

[29]This and the following quote: Burlyn Michel to Govindjee; personal communication [email], 27 November 2007.

Figure III.4: Warburg, sitting in the shade of a tree. In the white T-shirt is Martin (Marty) Schwartz, one of Warburg's junior co-authors; next to Schwartz (far right in photo, with a band-aid on his arm) is the physiologist George Wald, who had worked together with Warburg, before, in 1934, he went to Harvard University. (This photograph was taken by Burlyn Michel on July 22, 1949, on an island near Woods Hole, Massachusetts.)

> On June 22 we had another round between Warburg and Emerson. The new measurements of the Warburg group were presented by Dean Burk who said, or was it Warburg himself, that never have quantum yields been measured so accurately and definitively as at Bethesda (Burk's laboratory). [...] Not only have Warburg's results been confirmed as expected but it was seriously contested that quantum numbers of 3 have theoretical significance. Emerson, of course, showed numerous experiments evidently proving that no change in procedure will bring the quantum yield below the conventional 0.1. Most among the lay audience were inclined to believe Warburg who stated that the matter was settled and that Emerson's data were wrong.[30]

Emerson himself mentioned the meeting one month later in a letter to William Arnold, written on 21 July, 1949 – apparently still in a gloomy state of mind:

[30]Quoted in Kamen (1985), p. 304.

Dear Bill: I was sorry you didn't come to Woods Hole, but glad to pick up some news about you from [Stanley] Holt. I hope he gave you a good report of the meetings. I wish I knew what your opinion is now concerning the quantum yield of photosynthesis. Burk regards the matter as settled in Warburg's favor. I am unable to put my finger on any error in the Burk–Warburg experiments which would appear to account for the discrepancy between their results and mine, but as (James) Franck says, there are a number of things about their experiments which are "very fishy". I felt it wasn't much use to discuss things with Burk, because to me he seemed inclined to conceal important points in a rather deceitful way. I dislike having a controversy with such people. Warburg doesn't speak to me at all anymore.[31]

Shortly after this last contest, Warburg returned to Berlin, where he succeeded in having his institute re-established as one of the newly founded Max Planck Institutes.

THE 1949 SCIENCE PAPER

The first paper to appear in print, documenting the outcome of Warburg's work with collaborators in the United States, was published in *Science* in September 1949 as Burk, Hendricks, Korzenovsky, Schocken & Warburg (1949). The paper started with a reminder of the measurements of Warburg & Negelein (1923), from which, as the authors put it *"it became clear that an unknown principle, active in nature, awaited elucidation by physics and chemistry"* (p. 225). These findings had been *"rediscovered"*, Burk et al. (1949) wrote, using an improved experimental setup: a two-vessel method, in which a slightly acidic, phosphate-containing buffer solution was used, while the light intensity was measured with the actinometer. (The use of a two-vessel technique was a response to the criticism raised by Emerson and Lewis (1941, 1943) who had asked that the changes in carbon dioxide and oxygen should be measured simultaneously, while the acidic medium remained unchanged.) Furthermore, a procedure was devised that, from the point of view of Burk et al. (1949), made all calculated corrections for respiration effects unnecessary: White light of undetermined intensity was used to illuminate the vessels from above, which was meant to ensure that the rate of photosynthesis was always far more intensive than the rate of respiration. An additional red beam of measured intensity then caused an increase in the rate of photosynthesis, which was manometrically recorded. This new set-up had the advantage, Burk et al. (1949) claimed, that *"the efficiency of the*

---

[31]Emerson to Arnold, 21 July 1949, Robert Emerson Papers, 1923-61, Record Series 15/4/28, Box 1, Folder: Arnold, William. University of Illinois Archives.

energy transformation has now been measured under the conditions of growth, so that very likely the experiments can be extended to any length of time" (p. 227). The authors concluded:

> *It follows from the data obtained that in the spectral region 630 to 660 mμ no more than 4 quanta are required to produce one molecule of oxygen gas. A requirement of 3 quanta is open to serious consideration, although thus far the average value in our experiments has been nearer 4 than 3.*[32]

The interesting fact is that in a carbonate buffer solution the minimum quantum requirement values measured by the Warburg group were 10.5, 9.8 and 11.3 – thus, nicely matching the measurements done at Urbana and elsewhere. The low values of 3.6 or 3.9 were only obtained in the acidic, phosphate-containing buffer solution. This did not go unnoticed, and Burk et al. (1949) commented on these measurements: *"It may be gathered from this example that the efficiency in the unnatural carbonate buffer is only a fraction of the efficiency in culture medium"* (p. 228). Finally an *"Addendum"* to the paper stated that quantum yield measurements had been demonstrated to, and carried out by, students of the physiology class at Woods Hole in July 1949: *"Requirements of 3 to 5 quanta per molecule of oxygen gas produced in photosynthesis were observed on these two days"* (p. 229). The message one could take from this addendum was that Warburg's methods, in fact, were so easy and straightforward that any student was able to reproduce his results; so that one could really not blame Warburg for the fact that Emerson seemed unable to do so.

This Science paper was widely read and received considerable attention. Burk, Warburg's man in the United States, wrote to his new master and mentor on 2 November 1949:

> *The Science article has been a grand success, and it is too bad that you have not been here to enjoy all the attention that has been paid to it. We have had an enormous number of requests for reprints from every corner of the country and every kind of laboratory, including, oddly enough, many hospital laboratories. There have been many popular write-ups, with more to come. News Week [sic] ran a column on it under the heading 'Battle of the Plants'. Industrial and News Edition of the American Chemical Society is planning a 3000 word lead article. Scientific Monthly has asked me to write an article on the subject, of general nature. Time Magazine is considering running an episode. Even the Washington Evening Star of last Thursday (eight weeks after appearance of the*

---

[32]Burk et al. (1949), p. 229.

article) ran a column on it, and described the work as 'one of the major scientific events of the year'.[33]

Public attention would not die down for a long time, as it was being constantly fanned by Burk's series of public speeches, which included his talk at the annual meeting of the American Association for the Advancement of Science (AAAS), which took place at the end of December 1949. In his speech Burk had framed Warburg's research in economic terms, and confronted his audience with a calculation of how much more energy could be retrieved through sunlight if the photosynthetic process could be exploited on an industrial scale. On 20 January 1950, Burk told Warburg that their work had made it to the front page of the New York Times (Burk sent off a copy of the newspaper). The pertinent story, which was written by the science journalist William L. Laurence, well-known owing to his former position as the official journalist of the Manhattan Project, started as follows: *"Vital forces found in plants may increase world's food: Scientists, reporting efficiency up to 87% in using energy of sunlight, visualize 100-fold rise in yield of algae".* German newspapers were soon to follow – with headlines such as *"More effective use of solar energy can multiply food production one hundred times"* (Neue Zeitung, 7. January 1950). Burk surely had reason to be content with the success of his public relation campaign.

THE 1950 BIOCHIMICA ET BIOPHYSICA ACTA PAPER

Already at this early stage, the controversy had taken on a note of mutual lack of trust, personal defamation and suspected dishonesty between the participants: Warburg seemed to have taken Emerson's critique as a personal slight, while Emerson in turn felt exceedingly offended by Warburg's dismissive attitude towards him. This situation was not alleviated by the second paper of the Warburg group, submitted in June 1949 to the Biochimica et Biophysica Acta (BBA) and that appeared in print as Warburg, Burk, Schocken & Hendricks (1950). The contents were very similar to the Science paper, although in an extended form, presenting methods and data in more detail. However, when reading the BBA paper, one gets the impression that Warburg and Burk were, in fact, intent on taking the controversy (which was, after all, centered on an item of data) to another level, namely, using scientific esteem and prestige as a weapon – for example, they richly decorated the paper with photographs that had no obvious relevance to the content but rather showed the authors at work or posing with a number of other eminent scientists, mainly Nobel laureates.

---

[33] Archive of the BBAW, NL Warburg 174. Burk to Warburg, 2 Nov. 1949.

Warburg et al. (1950) stated in this BBA paper that the established value of no more than 4 quanta of red light to produce one molecule of oxygen, had *"sometimes been doubted by theoreticians, and it is a fact that certain investigators have raised methodological objections"* (p. 335). Notwithstanding these critical voices, the authors strongly confirmed the accuracy of a minimum quantum requirement of 3 to 4 quanta per molecule oxygen; and that the so-called *"carbon dioxide burst"* only was due to frothing which occurred if the solution was inappropriately shaken. Finally, the authors made a point of stating that the quotient of CO_2/O_2 (i.e. γ), which they claimed to have monitored simultaneously, was between -0.8 and -1.3. This was presumably done to counter Emerson's criticism of variable γ values during experimentation, although neither Emerson's name, nor his paper, nor the specific point of critique received a mention.

It was only in the appendix that the paper dealt explicitly with the objections raised by Emerson and Lewis. Warburg et al. (1950) described that Emerson and Lewis had used a carbonate-bicarbonate buffer solution only in order to escape the difficulties that were encountered when using a phosphate buffer solution (notably, the carbon dioxide burst!), and that Emerson and Lewis believed that the actual photosynthetic quantum yield was the same in both solutions. Warburg et al. (1950) complained, however, that no data had been provided by Emerson and Lewis to substantiate this statement. They wrote:

> *We can confirm Emerson's finding that in the carbonate-bicarbonate mixtures the quantum requirement is 10 to 12, but we cannot confirm that the same quantum efficiency is obtained in the acid culture medium. [...] Maximum yields should therefore not be determined in the carbonate mixture, as has been done frequently during the last 10 years.*[34]

THE PAPER IN ARCHIVES OF BIOCHEMISTRY

This point was further elaborated in a third paper, Warburg & Burk (1950*b*), which was published in the Archives of Biochemistry in January 1950. Therein, Warburg and Burk maintained the following:

> *[T]he proposed 'CO$_2$ outburst', at variance with the experience of the previous century and a half, was never actually demonstrated in published experiments involving quantum yield measurements. In the only completely detailed efficiency experiment in which the light-dark time course was repeated [cited Emerson & Lewis (1939), p. 4], a calculation, not performed by the authors,*

---

[34]Warburg et al. (1950), p. 346.

shows that the pressure changes for the second 5-minute periods of illumination were actually more positive (less negative) than for the first 5-minute periods [...]. This result, offered as a typical experimental example, was a direct contradiction of an outburst.[35]

Getting this paper published in the Archives had not been an easy task. On 18 December 1949, Burk informed Warburg that *"after some difficulty"* the paper had been accepted, although the editors had recommended that the referees' advice for revision be followed.[36] Burk wrote a letter of explanation to the editor (which had the intended success) and changed nothing.[37] However, Burk was not sure how to address the problem of Emerson's values; until then he would have firmly endorsed Warburg's notion that inadequate shaking had irreversibly harmed Emerson's cultures, while now Burk thought that he had some evidence to suggest that the shaking might, after all, not be so important. Burk's solution was characteristic of his general attitude towards the controversy:

I think we should be careful not to indicate that Emerson's 'Emerson Effect' was due only to inadequate shaking on his part, even though that might indeed be one way to produce such an apparent effect. The less said specifically about Mr. Emerson, the better I believe.[38]

On the whole Burk was enthusiastic about this piece of work: *"The more I read the article, the more I like it, everything is so beautifully clear and well organized, and it is a classic in its way,"* he wrote to Warburg. It is worth noting that this paper was written after the 1949 book "Photosynthesis in Plants" had appeared, edited by Franck together with the plant physiologist Walter E. Loomis (1898–1977), in which, for example, William Arnold's paper was published.[39] Warburg & Burk (1950*b*)

---

[35]Warburg & Burk (1950*b*), p. 413.

[36]The anonymous referee's report is preserved in the Burk–Warburg correspondence; see the sheet dated November 9, 1949, in the Archive of the BBAW, NL Warburg 174. Publication was recommended, despite the fact that the paper was very one-sided. Summarising experimental results rather than writing them out in detail was requested. Of particular interest is the following statement: *"The emphasis that these experiments have been conducted by students in the physiology class appears unfair to those who have had experience with students and who know how easily younger people can be influenced by a strong personality. This should not be taken as a criticism of the experiments as such, but it appears to me absolutely unfair to quote any inexperienced person in support of work which even an experienced investigator has great difficulty in forming a clear picture of the essential points which may modify his results".*

[37]Burk's reply is likewise preserved; see Archive of the BBAW, NL Warburg 174.

[38]This and the following quote: Archive of the BBAW, NL Warburg 174. Burk to Warburg, 18 Dec. 1949.

[39]See Franck & Loomis (1949). In a letter to Emerson of 1947, Franck explained the underlying idea of this volume as follows: "My cooperation with Dr. Loomis came

directly addressed the challenge raised in this 1949 publication: *"The results reported in this volume seemed to be conclusive and final: with three different and independent methods – manometric, polarographic, and calorimetric – minimum quantum requirements of 10-12/molecule of O_2 produced were obtained"* (p. 414). However, Warburg and Burk were determined to contest these results based on their experimental findings at high light intensities, the many advantages of which they discussed at length (pp. 419–421). Nine experiments were described in detail; again, in their only attempt to use a carbonate buffer solution, Warburg & Burk (1950*b*) faithfully reproduced Emerson's quantum yield values.[40] The authors conceded this phenomenon, yet again drew attention to the fact that it only occurred in a medium that they found unacceptable because of its alkaline conditions: *"In no experiment in carbonate buffer at pH 9 have we observed lower quantum values than 8, the average being about 10"* (p. 441). In a large table at the end of the paper, Warburg & Burk (1950*b*) finally detailed the values of γ produced in their experiments, which was defined as CO_2 absorbed/O_2. The γ values were in the range from -0.8 to -1.33, with an average of -1.06; these deviations, the authors pointed out, were totally at variance with what Emerson and Lewis had claimed, since, as far as they were concerned, there was no indication of anything like a carbon dioxide burst:

> On average a little more CO_2 was absorbed in the light than O_2 was produced. Thus, one of the two main loopholes that have been used to evade the high efficiency in photosynthesis is now closed. [...] The fact must thus be envisaged that in a perfect nature photosynthesis is perfect too.[41]

It is hardly surprising that Warburg (together with Burk) and Emerson no longer communicated directly with one another. However, after the publication of the paper in Science, Emerson had turned to the

---

about through his insistence and because I agreed with him several years ago that it would be desirable to mildly expose even the plant physiologists at this time to the fact that it might be advantageous for them to learn a little bit about the basic facts of photosynthesis. After all it should not be entirely unimportant to them, and his idea was to do it according to the well known principle, 'How do I present the facts of life to my child?'. I cannot overcome the fear that we may not have any greater success than parents usually have in that case. [...] Gaffron, of course, balks every time we discuss the matter. He insists that it is foolish to think that 'apple growers' should be able to understand anything beyond the market price of apples." Franck to Emerson, 29 Jan. 1947, Robert Emerson Papers, 1923-61, Record Series 15/4/28, Box 1, Folder: Franck, James, University of Illinois Archives.

[40]Cf. "Experiment No. 2", Warburg & Burk (1950*b*), pp. 432-433.

[41]Warburg & Burk (1950*b*), p. 413.

plant physiologist Sterling B. Hendricks (1902–1981; one of Warburgs co-authors in this series of papers), whom Emerson knew from earlier years, and asked him how he could possibly have joined forces with Warburg and Burk. Burk wrote in a letter to Warburg, on 18 December, that he had spent Thursday evening with Hendricks, helping him to answer Emerson's letter:

> [Emerson] spent many crocodile tears in the letter over the fact that Hendricks had ever had the misfortune to get himself tied up with such "dishonest" work as ours, in which many unsupported claims were made, and in which many formerly claimed virtues of procedure were now relinquished without explanation: settling of cells, low intensity, slow gas stream etc. Then Emerson went on to say that our cell concentration was now too great to be properly handled by the kinds of vessels we used. (You remember in his 1949 book article he had complained otherwise, that you had earlier used too small a number of cells?) Well, now there are too many, according to him, to even get good respiration readings. [...] Hendricks did not try to answer many of the detailed points, but told Emerson he thought they were all minor, and that he ought, if interested, to try and find something wrong in major principle, if he could! So Emerson is, as we fully expected, up to his old tricks. But he won't get far.[42]

It is worth taking a look at this from the other side of the dispute. Emerson wrote the following letter in response to a report of Burk's presentation at the AAAS meeting at the end of December 1949 by the plant physiologist Frederick C. Steward:

> Dear Mr. Steward,
>
> I appreciated receiving your account of Burk's performance in New York. One of our graduate students was there, too, and gave us his impressions, but the field is so new to him that he couldn't give us as full an account as you do. We are amused that Burk had no time for discussion of results with scientific colleagues, but had plenty of time to spill a big story for newspaper reporters. [...]
>
> Yes, Burk gives one this impression that he is making an intentional effort to confuse issues, rather than to clarify them. I'm inclined to agree that an ethical problem is involved, as well as a question of scientific fact. I'll appreciate advice on how to deal with the ethical issue, but I'm inclined to let it go until we have settled the facts.
>
> With best wishes,

---

[42] Archive of the BBAW, NL Warburg 174. Burk to Warburg, 2 Nov. 1949.

Sincerely, Robert Emerson.[43]

4   FRANCK'S ATTEMPT TO FIND A COMPROMISE

While Emerson struggled to find errors in Warburg's experimental procedure and his calculation method, Franck chose a different strategy. He was ready to grant Warburg that his data and methods were as sound as Emerson's, yet Franck suggested that these data did not reflect the maximum yield of actual photosynthesis. On 14 March 1949, when Warburg was still in Bethesda, Franck sent Warburg a manuscript to look at, with the following remark:

> *I would be so glad if you could subscribe to the view that the differences between the findings in the quantum yield rather indicate a difference in the observed photochemical processes than to some measurement error on the part of the observer.*[44]

Franck wanted to publish this hypothesis and, was, therefore, interested in hearing what Warburg had to say. Two weeks later, Warburg answered rather briefly that he had studied the paper but, of course, could not agree; furthermore, Warburg did not want it mentioned in the paper that he had read the manuscript, since people might then assume that he supported the paper's argument. However, Warburg concluded the letter on a warm note: *"Finally, I have to say how very glad I was about our latest reunion. Our last meeting was in Berlin, at the Physical Society, seventeen years ago, when you made your unforgettable speech in memory of my father."*[45]

Franck's paper was published shortly thereafter, as Franck (1949) in the Archives of Biochemistry. Therein he briefly reviewed the disagreement, describing how Emerson and Lewis explained Warburg's earlier measurements: namely, that in a phosphate-containing, acidic medium a burst of carbon dioxide was observed, which resulted in apparent values of very low quantum requirement of oxygen evolution – possibly even lower than 4 – since the carbon dioxide release was erroneously taken for the photosynthetic formation of oxygen. This explanation, Franck underlined, had become widely accepted in the United States. However, Franck also mentioned that, in the meantime, Warburg had rejected

---

[43]Emerson to Professor F.C. Steward January 28th, 1950; Botany Department; University of Rochester; Rochester 3, New York. Letter kindly provided by David Walker.

[44]MPG Archiv, III. Abt., Rep. 1, Nr. 195. Franck to Warburg, 11 March 1949. Original letter in German; translation by one of the authors (KN).

[45]MPG Archiv, III. Abt., Rep. 1, Nr. 195. Warburg to Franck, 28. March 1949. Original letter in German; translation by one of the authors (KN).

Emerson's criticism and reconfirmed his values under rather different experimental conditions. Franck continued:

> *The present writer, who was privileged to have oral discussions with Warburg and with Emerson, finds it hard to accept the point of view that only Warburg's method under special conditions will permit the algae to reduce CO_2 with a quantum yield of 1/4 when all other observations systematically give 1/10 as the highest value. On the other hand, it is not certain that the occurrence of the Emerson effect [i.e. the CO_2 outburst] is the main cause of the difference between Emerson's and Warburg's new results, because this effect, while undoubtedly present in both observations, seems to be smaller in Warburg's new experiments than in Emerson's.*[46]

From Franck's point of view, the difference by a factor of two between the values of the two parties seemed too high to be entirely due to the confounding factor identified by Emerson and Lewis; furthermore, Franck saw some evidence pointing to the fact that Warburg's findings might not only be quantitatively different from those of other groups but also qualitatively. Franck's suggestion, then, was intended to reconcile the results of Emerson's and Warburg's measurements, under the assumption that respiration might be interfering with the different processes of photosynthesis – in particular under conditions where the latter is not much higher than the former, that is, around the compensation point, at very low light intensities:

> *We introduce the assumption that Warburg's high quantum yield may be connected with the reduction of respiratory intermediates rather than with the reduction of CO_2. That is possible because Warburg's measurements are carried out under conditions where the photosynthetic rates are smaller than or, at best, comparable to, the respiration rates.*[47]

Although other researchers had suspected that respiration interfered with photosynthesis, Franck held that no systematic attempt had been made to explore the consequences of this observation; he was convinced that his approach was *"not only able to reconcile Warburg's quantum measurements with those of others, but also agrees with results of an entirely different nature"* (p. 298). In particular, Franck suggested that, instead of using CO_2, the reducing agents of photosynthesis might be utilized, under certain conditions, to reduce half-oxidized respiratory intermediates:

---

[46] Franck (1949), p. 298.
[47] Franck (1949), p. 299.

Thus, every half-oxidized molecule reduced photochemically will prevent the consumption of one-half molecule of oxygen by respiration. The evolution of CO_2 will be diminished by a whole molecule. In other words, the process would add one oxygen molecule and take away one CO_2 molecule from the balance sheet of respiration for every 4 quanta absorbed by the photosynthetic apparatus.[48]

Franck pointed to then recent findings that indicated a strong affinity of chlorophyll to the acid respiratory intermediates, if only they were able to enter the chloroplast. He suspected that Warburg's experimental conditions might result in an abnormal permeability of the chloroplast membrane, which would allow respiratory intermediates to enter these organelles in great quantities. The culture's age might be one of those factors, prolonged anaerobicity another factor, and so forth.

Yet, after having developed this argument in rather sophisticated terms, Franck (1949) conceded, in a *"Note added in proof"*, that in light of the experimental conditions used by Warburg, Burk and others at Woods Hole, this theory of his had become obsolete – because in the Woods Hole experiments, the yield remained high even under conditions where photosynthesis exceeded respiration several times, thanks to the combination of white background illumination with a red beam of measured intensity. In addition to that, at very low carbon dioxide concentration levels in the vessel, illumination with the red beam apparently *"did not measurably change the oxygen consumption of normal respiration"* (p. 312). Far from being frustrated, Franck observed:

However the present author is still convinced that the above discussion contains a good deal of material useful for the reconciliation of the differences in the results of quantum yields and of the chemical nature of intermediates of photosynthesis. He believes that there are two different photosynthetic processes, one with the quantum yield of 1/4 , the other with 8 quanta [i.e., the quantum yield of 1/8] and that the former is exceptional, taking place only when the chloroplast membranes become permeable, thus permitting mutual interactions between photosynthesis and respiration. High acidity, which discharges acids, is obviously one of the conditions necessary for the occurrence of that process.

If, as the new experiments indicate, the replacement of CO_2 reduction by that of half-oxidized respiration products is not responsible for the higher quantum yield process observed by Warburg, it might be that a part of the energy of respiration can be used for photosynthetic processes. [...] [I]t might be possible that the energy stored in the phosphate bonds produced by respiration might be transferred to

---

[48] Franck (1949), p. 300.

phosphate bonds of the CO_2 complex and of intermediate products of photosynthesis. In that way, the energy of 12 K-cal. would be available in the molecules to be reduced before each photochemical reaction and, with that additional energy photosynthesis may proceed with 4 quanta. However, this photosynthesis could, even if all other conditions are favorable to it, only proceed to a maximum rate of 1.5 times that of respiration. Any photosynthesis in algae beyond 1.5 times respiration would need 8 quanta [per oxygen evolved].[49]

The idea that back reactions might be involved, which, to some extent, linked respiration and photosynthesis, or, alternatively, that the energy gained from respiratory processes was used for photosynthetic carbon dioxide reduction, would be around for the next few decades and would become very influential. In fact, even though Warburg himself would have shuddered at this thought, one could claim that this idea became a major source of inspiration for Warburg and Burk's later photosynthesis model, which became known as the *"one-quantum mechanism"* of photosynthesis, which we will turn to in a later chapter.

5 FURTHER EXCHANGE OF BLOWS

Although Emerson was in rather low spirits by the end of 1949, as one can take from his letters after the confrontation at Woods Hole (see p. 59), he was far from feeling defeated. In his letter to Steward of January 1950, partly quoted above, Emerson also outlined his future research plans:

As I may have suggested in my last letter to you, we are now pretty sure that the major cause of error in the Burk–Warburg work is their assumption [...] that there was no "physical lag" in their manometric system. On the basis of this unsupported assertion (which we find to be strictly contrary to fact), they based most of their photosynthesis measurements on 10-minute exposures to light, alternated with 10-minute intervals of either darkness or unmeasured light. This does not lead to correct values of photosynthesis in either phosphate or carbonate buffer solutions. However, there are additional factors in their work which are still obscure, and we shall not be satisfied until we can give a quantitative explanation of all the major inconsistencies. We do make progress toward this objective, but it's disappointingly slow.[50]

---

[49]Franck (1949), p. 313.

[50]Emerson to Professor F.C. Steward January 28th, 1950; Botany Department; University of Rochester Rochester 3, New York. Letter kindly provided by David Walker..

Emerson pursued this line of research with his assistant Shimpe Nishimura and with Charles Whittingham, a research associate from the University of Cambridge, England, who was spending a year at Urbana.[51] Emerson presented the results of their common work at a symposium on "Carbon Dioxide Fixation and Photosynthesis", organized in July 1950 by the Society for Experimental Biology and hosted by the Biochemistry Department of the University of Sheffield, England. The conference was attended by all the major players in the field of photosynthesis, including, among others, Burk, Emerson, Franck, French, Gaffron, Robin Hill, Bessel Kok, Daniel Arnon and Melvin Calvin. This range of excellent speakers was complemented by some renowned figures from the discipline of biochemistry, such as Hans Krebs (1900–1981) and Harland G. Wood (1907–1991), who were working on the phenomena of carbon dioxide fixation in heterotrophs. Warburg was also expected to attend, although he failed to show up at the last minute. Emerson gave a detailed report of his journey to Europe in a letter of 3 November 1950 to the physicist Louis N. Ridenour (1911–1959); Burk also wrote a relatively long letter to Warburg about the Sheffield symposium. Thus, the event is well documented by both sides.

According to these letters, the largest part of a full day of the symposium was devoted to the discussion of the minimum quantum requirement of photosynthesis, with the center stage being given to Emerson's and Burk's presentations. According to his letter to Ridenour, Emerson was very satisfied with his experience there. He was extremely pleased by the attitude of the audience, as he pointed out:

> *Close attention was given to both his [i.e. Burk's] remarks and mine. It was a pleasure to speak to an audience which was so clearly willing to give its attention to the experimental details that have come to play such an important part in this controversy. The groups to which I have spoken in the U.S. have always betrayed a certain irresponsibility about following the reasoning from experiment to conclusion. People want to know what my conclusions are, but they don't want to take the trouble of tracing the conclusions back to the observations upon which they are based. They usually take the attitude that Emerson probably knows how to do his experiments, and it is not their responsibility to understand his reasons for preferring one sequence of operations to another. The Sheffield audience was clearly willing to take its own responsibility for reasoning from experimental evidence to conclusion.*

---

[51] At Cambridge, Whittingham was a close collaborator of Robin Hill's, with whom he published in 1955 a small monograph on photosynthesis; see Hill & Whittingham (1955).

Emerson then continued to describe the course of events:

> *[George E.] Briggs did a careful job of steering the discussion, and of giving opportunity for expression of all viewpoints. Burk was asked to give his opinion regarding the criticisms of his work, which were implied by the tests of his methods reported from our laboratory. At first, he tried to avoid comment, but questioners were insistent, and he finally said there seemed to him to be nothing in our work, which he would not be able to explain in a few days' time. I think it is fair to say that the consensus of opinion was that he had failed to prove his case.*[52]

It is interesting to compare Emerson's letter with the letter that Burk wrote to Warburg immediately after the Sheffield symposium. Needless to say, his account diverged quite widely from Emerson's. Burk wrote:

> *Veni, vidi, but not quite vici. The Philistines were present in great numbers, including all our old "friends" who surpassed themselves in their attempts to muddy the waters without any new experiments. Emerson talked as in Chicago 1947, Urbana 1948, Woods Hole 1949 style, followed by a pecking at our large Archives article and finally by just one slide of new data, with the 2-vessel method in which he claimed that he could now get 4 quanta for certain time periods but 8 quanta if he took 30' periods and included the first 5-10 minutes. In other words, almost but not quite a confirmation yet, but a marked change, nevertheless, as [Daniel] Arnon rose to point out.*[53]

Burk's admission that he had not quite "won" strongly supports Emerson's impression that Burk had failed to convince the audience. It is also interesting to observe that Burk saw the situation as a matter of victory versus defeat, while Emerson, by contrast, mentioned a lack of proof. It also seems that Burk had failed to grasp Emerson's point, since the latter had in fact attempted to show under which circumstances one would get the (artifactually) high quantum yield, while Burk only picked at the fact that Emerson did not present any "new" data. In the remainder of the letter, Burk emphasized that everybody in Sheffield was greatly disappointed that Warburg had not shown up, and that people kept asking Burk whether Warburg might, perhaps, make it after all. Burk had

---

[52]Emerson to Ridenour, 3 Nov. 1950, Robert Emerson Papers, 1923-61, Record Series 15/4/28, Box 1, Folder: Graduate College Correspondence, University of Illinois Archives. Note that George E. Briggs (1893–1985) was Professor of Botany at Cambridge University.

[53]This and the following quote: Archive of the BBAW, NL Warburg 174. Burk to Warburg, 10 July 1950.

also shown photographs of the Dahlem laboratory during his talk, which, he thought, greatly impressed everybody – most of the participants had assumed that the institute was still in ruins. Burk proudly boasted: *"I think it made the old-time Berliners homesick and the British and American keenly interested."*

The contributions that were discussed at length in Sheffield were published one year later in a 1951 conference volume. Emerson's contribution, published as Nishimura, Whittingham & Emerson (1951), clearly explained why the two-vessel method, used by Warburg and his co-workers for their quantum yield measurements, was extremely sensitive to significant systematic errors. Even tiny aberrations, which in the one-vessel method would be trifling, were likely to have enormous consequences on the final result. As Nishimura et al. (1951) argued in great detail, slight errors in the individual manometer readings – errors of no more than 0.3 mm, which were bound to occur all the time – could dramatically change the calculated values of γ, which, in turn, severely altered the resulting quantum yield. They identified the most dramatic source of error as being the fact that, in contrast to the long established practice, Warburg and Burk had failed to take into account the time interval for a physical lag in the response of the manometer to the change from light to darkness and from dark to light. While Warburg and Burk had claimed that in their experiments *"mixing was so efficient that there was no physical lag in the response of the manometer to the successive light and dark periods"*, from the point of view of Nishimura et al. (1951), there was clear evidence that a physical lag occurred and that it had substantial effects on the readings (p. 194). Consequently, they concluded that the measurements provided by Warburg and his associates failed to demonstrate the high efficiencies, which they reported. Nishimura et al. (1951) were not impressed either by the values for γ provided by Warburg and his co-workers in their various articles, which were always near -1: if the value was calculated separately for light and dark periods, as Nishimura et al. (1951) demonstrated, large deviations from -1 were revealed.

In view of the technical difficulties inherent in manometric techniques, which they clearly brought to the fore, it is surprising that Nishimura et al. (1951) still thought that the method was indispensable (p. 178). They argued that the two-vessel measurements should be developed with a differential manometer and with the simultaneous illumination of both vessels (at the time, the two vessels to be compared had to be measured one after another, which, of course, increased the likelihood of experimental errors). Thus, only the 'new' suggested method would allow for readings to be taken with the required degree of precision. In their

74

conclusion, Nishimura et al. (1951) made the following comment on Warburg's strategy of experimentation and argument:

> *We find in Warburg & Burk's data no evidence to persuade us that their specifications for obtaining highest efficiencies of photosynthesis are significant, regardless of what future experiments may prove. We note that some of their specifications are directly contradictory to the requirements emphasized by Warburg up to 1947. They mention the use of chloride in the culture solution, the importance of growing the cells in unsterilized medium prepared with well water, the avoidance of sedimentation, the temperature of 20° C being favourable for highest efficiency, etc. We find in the papers of Warburg & Negelein (1922, 1923) and of Warburg (1947) quite other specifications for obtaining highest efficiency. No chloride was added to the culture medium, and it was categorically stated that sedimentation during culture growth did not affect photosynthetic efficiency adversely. A temperature of 10° C was specified as essential for obtaining maximum efficiency. Up to 1947, it was stated that shaking the cells in a manometer vessel results in progressive damage, and ultimately in zero photosynthesis. In 1950 it is stated that cells are only damaged by shaking in darkness, and that they may be shaken indefinitely in the light without suffering injury. In no case are these specifications supported by experimental evidence. Possibly they represent only ad hoc assumptions.*[54]

What Emerson did not include in this paper was his own nagging suspicion that, although he was reasonably sure that Warburg and Burk's methods were flawed, he was not yet fully in control of the situation. This can clearly be seen to be the case in the following letter that Emerson wrote to Gaffron on 4 April 1950, which also nicely illustrates the many practical difficulties of making quantum yield measurements, beginning with the problem of mounting the appropriate source of light:

> *It still seems to us that difference in physical lag [...] is likely to be the most important source of systematic error, but we have spells of worrying that there is something else which we have not thought of yet. One can get quantum requirements of 4 without too much difficulty, but we are not yet able to get this result regularly, combined with a γ value close to unity, as Warburg and Burk claim to have done. I suspect the trick is to have just the right combination of CO_2 burst and physical lag. The errors from these two factors seem to work in opposite directions, when you use Burk–Warburg vessel volumes and 10'light-10'dark cycles without allowing any interval for physical lag.*

---

[54]Nishimura et al. (1951), p. 209.

The light source is still causing us concern. After months of effort to get two vessels equally illuminated by fluorescent lamps, we gave it up, and tried to produce two equal beams. Individual vessels differ too much to get equality from a surface illuminated by fluorescent lights. Also, we were worried that the Burk–Warburg results might depend on having only a small spot illuminated.

We made a nice beam-splitter with a ribbon filament lamp, and were able to adjust the two beams to equality within less than 1 per cent, but the infrared could not be filtered out well enough to permit use of the actinometer. So we gave up the ribbon filament, and are trying to do the same thing with a little cadmium lamp. This gives barely enough energy, and is sufficiently free of infrared, but its life-time is very short, and the energy keeps dropping from hour to hour. Sometimes I'm at my wit's end to think how to get around all the difficulties.[55]

6 CONTROVERSIAL THEMES AROUND 1950

This was the state of the debate around 1950. As is obvious from the course of events, interest in the question of the minimal quantum requirement or maximum quantum yield was still exceedingly high among photosynthesis researchers. In 1941, Franck and others had been convinced that the question had been settled in favor of quantum requirements approximating 10 to 12 quanta per molecule of oxygen evolved. One reads, for example, in the paper Franck & Herzfeld (1941): *"All theoretical considerations about the chemical nature of the intermediate products of photosynthesis and all thermochemical conclusions, therefore, have to be radically changed, since the number of photochemical steps and correspondingly, the energy balance is changed by a factor of 2 to 3"* (p. 978). However, in view of Warburg's reaction after 1945, the photosynthesis researchers were no longer so sure.

The controversy was definitely influenced, to some extent, by factors "outside" scientific boundaries *sensu stricto*. Warburg was a Nobel laureate, with a well-founded reputation as being an excellent experimenter, mastering manometry to the point of perfection; Emerson was considerably younger, far less famous, and, although he was hardly less proficient than Warburg in manometry, he had learned his technique in Warburg's laboratory, so that he always carried the stamp of a "disciple of", with the obvious connotation of inferiority. These were the circumstances upon which Warburg and Burk never failed to dwell, in order to gain maximum advantage for their views; furthermore, Burk was not averse

---

[55]Emerson to Gaffron, 4 April 1950, Robert Emerson Papers, 1923-61, Record Series 15/4/28, Box 1, Folder: Gaffron, Hans, University of Illinois Archives.

to using other unpleasant rhetorical tricks. Warburg and Burk constantly only referred to Franck as the main opponent to Warburg's work. As a quantum physicist, Franck allegedly argued on theoretical grounds only, while Warburg himself let Nature speak. If Emerson was mentioned at all, he was usually belittled, e.g., in Warburg, Geleick & Briese (1952), Emerson was introduced as a "botanist" (in other words, as someone who could not possibly know much about manometry). However, while their influence cannot be disputed, it is not so clear how far these factors actually drove the course of events. It is obvious that the general public, manipulated by journalists who had been thoroughly worked on by Burk (and who were more interested in crisp headlines than in going through dull experimental details), tended to think that Warburg was right and that the matter had been settled once and for all in his favor. And to a certain extent this also held true for the scientific public not involved in photosynthesis research. Yet, even the "inner circle" of scientists, who were actually engaged with the subject matter, many of whom were on excellent terms with Emerson, gave serious consideration to the new arguments brought forward by Warburg and Burk – not because of Warburg's reputation, but because the question was so important and the answer so obscure. The experiments from which the value had to be derived were so delicate that anyone could err, Warburg as well as Emerson. It is only obvious with hindsight that the "accurate" value (of 8 to 12 light quanta per molecule of oxygen) had been around since the start of the controversy in 1939. It was, in particular, two factors that potentially confounded the results: the condition of the algae cultures and the effect of respiration. It was already clear then that both factors decisively influenced the outcome of manometric experiments (although it was far less clear to what extent and in which ways) and it was known that the combined effects of these factors with other parameters, such as light intensity or temperature, might yield further unforeseeable consequences. Emerson and Lewis had positively established all this in 1939. Yet, being aware of the difficulties did not mean that they had been resolved.

The choice of the culture medium was another factor that influenced the outcome, although it was much easier to control the medium than the internal, physiological state of algae cultures or the obscure interfering effects of respiration. We have repeatedly emphasized that the choice of an acidic phosphate-containing buffer solution (preferred by Warburg and Burk) versus an alkaline, carbonate-bicarbonate buffer solution (preferred by Emerson) was significant. Emerson and Lewis had provided ample evidence that the use of an acidic buffer solution favored the development of a carbon dioxide burst, which tended to distort the experimental findings towards apparently lower quantum requirements. Warburg, on the other hand, argued that only the lowest possible quantum requirement was of theoretical importance. He had no trouble reproducing the values arrived at by Emerson and others using an alkaline medium; yet, Warburg held that, since the lowest numbers could only be obtained using a phosphate buffer solution, the measurements taken in carbonate-bicarbonate buffer solutions were useless. From Warburg's point of view, the higher values in an alkaline medium were caused by the fact that the algae were unable to photosynthesize properly at higher pH values. It has already been pointed out – e.g. in Govindjee (2001) – that, initially at least, Emerson and Warburg did not argue about the values measured in a carbonate-bicarbonate buffer solution. However, this situation changed in 1952, when Burk announced that the same low quantum yield had been measured in new carbonate mixtures;[56] we shall return to this problem (see p. 92). The issue remained controversial, so that around 1950 Emerson's priority was to establish once and for all that the data obtained in an alkaline buffer solution were as valid as the data arrived at using an acidic medium.

Returning to the physiological state of the algae as one of the main confounding factors mentioned earlier, one can clearly see from the correspondence between the major players how deeply they were preoccupied by this problem. Cultivating the algae had top priority, and was one of the most time-consuming activities in photosynthesis laboratories of that time period – indeed, Emerson employed a person specifically for that purpose, while he closely corresponded with the most knowledgeable algae experts of the time, such as the phycologist Ernst Pringsheim (1881–1970). Standard strains were eagerly exchanged between photosynthesis laboratories, as well as those strains of algae with which standard experiments – such as the Emerson and Arnold flashing light experiments of 1932 – had been carried out. This was the only way to try and approximate the homogeneity condition of experimental research with regard to the algae factor. However absurd Warburg's claims might look at first sight, for example, his complaints that he was unable to work with Emerson's cultures, since they had been improperly grown, these concerns were not totally unfounded. Emerson himself had established that the type of tap water used for the culture medium (Urbana versus Baltimore tap water) considerably changed the experimental results; this suggested that growing the algae at a very special location, such as on a north-facing Berlin-Dahlem windowsill, as Warburg claimed in Urbana, might also exert some decisive influence on the algae's photosynthetic performance. (Note, however, that it was later claimed in Warburg, Krip-

---

[56]For the pertinent publications, see Warburg et al. (1952) and Warburg (1952).

pahl & Schröder (1956) (p. 237) that the most efficient cultures were grown in pleasant summer temperatures, on a south-facing windowsill, which makes one have misgivings about the established causal relevance of one location over another.) Indeed, the subject was so complicated that by 1950 many were inclined to believe that almost any factor connected with algae culturing might influence the eventual quantum yield of photosynthesis.

The problem of respiration multiplied these uncertainties still further. Basic manometry was unable to differentiate qualitatively between the different kinds of gases that were produced or consumed. And although more sophisticated approaches that tried to amend this deficiency eventually became available (such as the two-vessel method), in the case of photosynthesis the matter was further complicated by the fact that respiration likewise involved changes in the volumes of oxygen and carbon dioxide; and it was also beyond question that respiration continued in the light, so that the rate of photosynthesis somehow had to be distinguished from that of respiration. The usual assumption was that the rate of respiration was the same in the light and in darkness, so that the gas exchange values in the light could be corrected rather easily by subtracting the values for respiration measured in the dark. In addition, Emerson and Lewis, in the 1940s, had tried to limit the risk of having the respiration rate change by using short intervals of light and darkness (which, however, had to be delicately balanced: if the intervals were too short, induction periods with their transient gas exchange phenomena tended to introduce measuring errors of another kind). From today's vantage point, it is clear that the fundamental assumption was inaccurate: light *does* influence the rate of respiration. However, scientists at the time were not so sure – all they knew was that the matter was uncertain and obscure. They acknowledged the problem and were clearly troubled by it, but no solution was at hand and, hence, they carried on their work without solving the issue. Gaffron, for example, wrote to Emerson on 4 March, 1950:

> *The 2-vessel method does not allow one to find out whether the respiratory quotient is changed during the exposure to light. What you obtain is always a composite figure. I am now worrying whether it may be possible that some queer intermediate products of photosynthesis are formed which at very low light intensities are preferentially burned again, replacing part or all of the ordinary dark metabolism. We then would have a special compensation reaction*

> *for which we have no proper correction in the measurements of the dark metabolism.*[57]

Emerson answered, on 4 April 1950:

> *If the respiratory quotient changes in the dark, then there is really no sense in trying to measure the quantum requirement at low light intensity. I agree with you that this is a possibility to be considered, but up to now we have all worked on the assumption that the respiration is not much changed by illumination. We should not give this up without good reason.*

Furthermore, there was the additional complication that respiration, as well as many other physiological processes in the cell, possibly interfered with photosynthesis in other ways than through gas exchange, such as, for example, the exchange of intermediate products. Perhaps there was a systematic interaction, but even if this was not the case, the risk of artificially induced interference, which is what Franck (1949) suspected, by the choice of cell treatment or other experimental conditions, clearly existed. These were serious concerns and nobody was able to rule out that any one of the plethora of metabolic side reactions and by-products of respiration and other processes under certain conditions interfered with (and confounded) the process of photosynthesis. By the end of the 1930s scientists were well aware that photosynthesis was a complex, flexible and highly adaptive process that was influenced by a vast number of factors, most of which were still unknown.

To cut a long story short: it was extremely difficult to judge the quantum requirement calculations of photosynthesis, based on experimental data with living cells; but this did not mean that it was impossible to make sound judgements. A quantum requirement of 8 to 12 had not only been measured manometrically, most prominently by Emerson and Rieke, but they had also been arrived at independently by other methods, such as microcalorimetry and polarography (the latter carried out by the biophysicist Frederick S. Brackett), which clearly was a fact in favor of these values. This was even conceded by Warburg himself. Yet even if this convergence of values decreased the odds that the Warburg–Negelein–Burk value was the accurate one, these other methods also faced enormous difficulties, so that the potential certainty that one could have expected from the confirmation of a value by different experimental approaches was, in this case, only moderate. And even with hindsight, one has to admit that a certain amount of skepticism was justified.

---

[57]This letter and the following quote: Robert Emerson Papers, 1923-61, Record Series 15/4/28, Box 1, Folder: Gaffron, Hans, University of Illinois Archives.

After all, even when mass spectroscopy became available, as the only reliable means to double-check the course of respiration in the light and in darkness, Allan H. Brown (1917–2004), the Madison-based expert in this technique, was unable to find any influence of light on respiration.[58]

Finally, we would like to draw attention to Warburg's strategy for dealing with Emerson's critique. Rabinowitch, in the obituary of Emerson, described this as follows:

> [T]he aim of finding a complete explanation of Warburg's results proved elusive, because Warburg, rather than investigating thoroughly the conditions under which the alleged high quantum yields could be obtained, kept publishing increasingly startling new observations, whose relation to his own earlier findings was not always clear, and which made Emerson's control experiments obsolete faster than they could be performed.[59]

The same point was already sarcastically commented on by Nishimura, Whittingham and Emerson in their 1951 paper (see quote above, p. 74). In his early studies, up to 1948, Warburg had emphasized that low light intensities had to be used in relatively short experiments, which led Franck to suggest that respiration was interfering with the apparent process; however, by 1950 Warburg claimed, together with Burk, that the highest efficiencies were obtained at high light intensities over long periods of time. Furthermore, in the early studies, very thick suspensions, which needed to be allowed to settle down in the vessel, had been recommended by Warburg, while he later favored the use of thin suspensions, which were rather vigorously shaken. Even the technique of supplementing a white background illumination with a red beam of measured intensity, introduced by Warburg and Burk in 1950 as the solution of the respiration problem, was dropped a few years later in favor of a "catalytic" amount of blue light, to which we shall return later. The concentration of carbon dioxide necessary for the highest yields was also slowly increased, up to 10 %.

These regular changes in experimental conditions lie at the core of the controversy. Warburg failed to demonstrate the actual causal relevance of the various factors implemented in his experiments; and this is why he finally lost his case. Nobody can blame Warburg for changing his original set-up in view of Emerson and Lewis's critique; but contrary to expectations, to conventions of scientific behavior and to

---

[58]The pertinent data were published in, e.g., Brown (1953) and Brown & Good (1955), although photosynthesis researchers knew of the data before this date, from talks and informal means of communication.

[59]Rabinowitch (1961), p. 123.

the requirements of methodology, Warburg never acknowledged that he had introduced changes as a consequence of appropriate criticism, well-founded comparative studies or other sound reasons. And neither did he produce sufficient evidence for the actual causal relevance of the new conditions. The changes that Warburg introduced to the set-up in later years appear completely arbitrary; they were done without any explanation being offered, and went from one extreme to the other – not to mention the fact that Warburg, Burk and their co-workers usually did not provide very precise descriptions of their set-up, even though the controversy was centered around these details. Emerson himself, as well as Rabinowitch, understandably interpreted this as a way of escaping criticism of the methods.[60] At the very least, it was strange that the range of experimental conditions used by Warburg and his co-workers did not evoke a matching range of experimental results. The quantum requirement of 2.8, at which Warburg finally settled, was not substantially lower than the value of 3 that Emerson and Lewis had already found in 1938, so that one might think – as Nishimura et al. (1951) did – that the variation of parameters was, after all, not as influential as Warburg had claimed.

The question remains, then, as to whether this controversy and the ensuing experimental research did anything to promote photosynthesis research. At first glance, the yield was meagre. Many financial and personal resources were consumed without the actual goal – settling the magical parameter – ever being reached. At second glance, however, these studies did result in much new knowledge being amassed, which became relevant in rather unforeseeable contexts (such as Emerson's finding of the "Red Drop", beyond 685 nm, in photosynthetic efficiency). The attempts to explain the differing results also led researchers to explore aspects of photosynthesis that had so far been neglected, such as the complex relationship between photosynthesis and respiration, and the intricate details of algae cultivation. However, after 1950 people started to lose interest in the debate, feeling that it had become stuck in a dead end. Warburg had failed to demonstrate the causally relevant factors in his set-up, and Emerson had inevitably been unable to prove them conclusively wrong. The shortcomings of the available methods – above all, the problems inherent in using manometry – had clearly been brought to the fore, so that, on this basis, a solution hardly seemed attainable. Nevertheless, the proponents would continue to struggle (unsuccessfully) for some years yet.

---

[60]On this point, see also the summary of the (inconsistent) conditions used by Warburg when demonstrating a quantum yield of 4 and less provided by Rabinowitch (1956), pp. 1947f.

Chapter IV

A HARDENING OF THE FRONTS

1 THE ONE-QUANTUM-MECHANISM

In the autumn of 1950, following an extended stay of Burk's at War-burg's institute in Berlin, Warburg and Burk outmatched themselves by proposing the so-called *"one-quantum mechanism"* of photosynthesis. This mechanism was first published in two short notes written in German – Warburg & Burk (1950*a*) and Warburg (1951) – while an extended version was presented in the form of a paper published in the Scientific Monthly, October 1951, as Burk, Cornfield & Schwartz (1951): "The efficient transformation of light into chemical energy in photosynthesis: An application of the Einstein Law of Photochemical Equivalence to living organisms".[1] It is interesting that, in the English-speaking world, this mechanism was first published in a semi-popular version; and it was only eight years later, in Warburg (1958), a (very disputed) review of photosynthesis research in Science, that the one-quantum mechanism made its way into a high-ranking journal for original papers.[2]

The contribution to the Scientific Monthly, by Burk et al. (1951), started with a derogatory account of Warburg's critics, in which, again, the names of the people involved were omitted and the pertinent publications not cited. The paper even failed to mention that it was Emerson who had initiated Warburg's visit to the United States, while many general and vague accusations were raised. The authors emphasized that the criticisms directed at Warburg and Burk were based purely on theoretical considerations, while there was no mention of objections against the ex-

---

[1]In this publication, Burk et al. (1951) claimed (e.g., p. 216) that Warburg had repeatedly discussed the problem of photosynthetic quantum yields with Einstein. However, no trace of such discussion seems to have survived. Thus, in view of the generally exaggerated style of the paper, it is doubtful that these discussions ever took place.

[2]See Warburg (1958). Note that there was considerable dismay among photosynthesis researchers following the publication of this very one-sided 1958 review of Warburg's. See, e.g., the letter by the photosynthesis researcher Norman E. Good to the biochemist Robin Hill, dated 2 January, 1959 (Cambridge University Library, Ms. Add. 9267/J.62):*"What did you think of this summer's article by Warburg on photosynthesis in Science? The general reaction in America was one of considerable irritation, in no small part irritation with the Editor of Science. The article was considered, rightly it seemed to me, as a mass of willful misrepresentation and as such not worthy of a reply. However, there are many profound regrets that scientists working in other fields should be so misinformed by a journal purporting to serve all scientists."*

perimental part of their work. Thus, most of the work done at Urbana and elsewhere was simply ignored, and the debate was distortedly featured as an argument between the open, experimental approach to science, in which Nature was allowed to speak for herself (represented by Warburg), and the anthropocentric pondering of the general possibilities, prejudiced by the then current physical theory (the approach allegedly taken by Warburg's opponents). Furthermore, Burk et al. (1951) reported that Warburg's opponents had claimed that a minimum of 10 to 20 quanta would be required to produce molecular oxygen, which was only true for the very first paper in the course of the debate, by Manning et al. (1938), while the usual alternative to Warburg's value of 3 to 4 were figures in the range of 8 to 10. One undoubtedly gains the impression that no attempt was made to present an impartial account of the disagreement; instead, the authors deliberately portrayed the events as a travesty, which favored Warburg's side of the story and made the outcome seem self-evident. Burk et al. (1951) then went on to celebrate the fact that the 4-quantum requirement had been finally confirmed beyond any doubt at Bethesda in 1949. No mention whatsoever was made of the critical responses to this value; instead, the authors continued to describe the developments that shortly before had taken place in Berlin, which were featured as a dramatic breakthrough:

> Although the four-quantum requirement was now definitely re-established, the fundamental mystery still remained, as to how four low-energy quanta could cooperate to yield high-energy carbohydrate in a manner that was in harmony with Einstein's photochemical equivalence law. If a single quantum of red light furnishes some 40,000 calories per mole, where do the missing 70,000 calories (110,000 – 40,000) come from? It was clear that some unknown principle of nature must be involved that would solve this "quantum riddle of photosynthesis" in a special manner. The answer to this riddle was finally obtained late in 1950 in continued joint investigation carried out in Berlin-Dahlem.[3]

The important phenomenon was, the authors reported, an effect that up to then had escaped everybody's notice: as the intervals of light and darkness were made increasingly shorter, down to one minute each, during the dark periods following a period of high light intensity a very large amount of oxygen disappeared from the system, ten times more than during normal respiration. Burk et al. (1951) explained this phenomenon as follows:

---

[3]This and the following quote: Burk et al. (1951), p. 216.

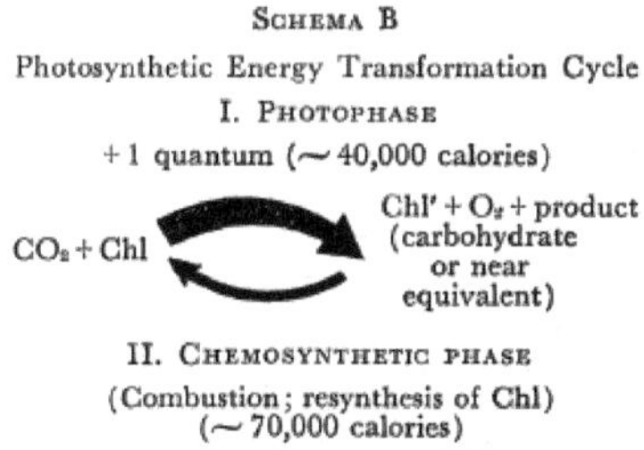

Schema B
Photosynthetic Energy Transformation Cycle
I. Photophase
+ 1 quantum ($\sim$ 40,000 calories)

CO_2 + Chl $\longrightarrow$ Chl' + O_2 + product (carbohydrate or near equivalent) $\longleftarrow$

II. Chemosynthetic phase
(Combustion; resynthesis of Chl)
($\sim$ 70,000 calories)

Figure IV.1: The "Photosynthetic Cycle" underlying the one-quantum mechanism. The scheme is described in Burk et al. (1951, p. 217) as follows: *"Chl represents the chlorophyll complex before illumination. Chl' is restored to Chl by the back reaction, at the expense of energy derived in the chemosynthetic reaction involving consumption of O_2 and product."*

It thus became obvious that the actual photochemical reaction is only detectable under conditions of rapid alternation of light and dark intervals, and why it had never been observed under conditions of continuous illumination. The oxygen consumption in the back reaction (most probably not identical with ordinary respiration) prevented one from seeing the full magnitude of the forward photochemical production of oxygen. The over-all process of photosynthesis clearly consists of two different reactions, which interlock cyclically and normally hide each other. One reaction is photochemical and proceeds in the light alone, and the other is a chemical oxidation reaction that goes on not only in the dark, but as further experimentation showed, in the light also.

This led the authors to the astonishing announcement that *"the quantum requirement was found under optimal conditions to be one"* (p. 216). The main idea was that the 70,000 missing calories were provided by back reactions that took place during the dark phase, in which two-thirds of the previously produced oxygen would be consumed in oxidation reactions. According to Burk et al. (1951), this also demonstrated that *"water as such is not an initial reactant"*, as most people by then believed (and as we still believe today), but rather entered photosynthesis during the dark reaction, which also provided the energy required for the decomposition of the water (p. 217). The energy thus released would then be used in the subsequent photophase, in which the complex of chlorophyll and a carbonic acid derivative would receive another 40,000 calories in the form of one absorbed quantum of red light. In summing up, then, 110,000 calories were available to produce actual carbohydrates and molecular oxygen. An integrated circle of dark and light reactions would require 3 light quanta, while the photochemical process alone needed 1 light quantum only (see Figure IV.1 for the original drawing of this cycle). The high rate of back reactions kept the efficiency at about 100 %. The culmination of the argument came when Burk et al. (1951) triumphantly exclaimed:

> *What could be simpler than that nature, in harmony with Einstein's photochemical equivalence law, has one molecule of chlorophyll absorb one quantum of light to reduce one molecule of CO_2 and produce one molecule of O_2?*[4]

These were the findings that Burk brought back to the United States when he returned at the end of January 1951 after his stay in Warburg's laboratory in Dahlem. Upon his return, Burk immediately assured Warburg that he would *"start the propaganda campaign in regard to the 1-quantum results"*, as quickly as possible.[5] This included him getting in touch again with his contact (William Laurence) at the New York Times, who had promised to feature the story prominently. Burk had also scheduled many talks; the first one would be in Pittsburgh (Pennsylvania) and would be entitled, *"The resolution of the quantum problem in photosynthesis"*. Burk, who had already sent off reprints of the German notes to all his friends and enemies, wrote: *"I hope that all of this activity will strike you as appropriate to the importance of the underlying work. It seems necessary and won't take too much time."* And, of course, Burk was also relieved to see that all his superiors at the NCI (National Cancer Institute) were so delighted with the paper on the photosynthesis mechanism, *"that from all signs no questions about 'cancer' will be asked, so there looks like no trouble here, on any such score"*. (This remark alluded to the fact that Burk had applied for a leave of absence with the declared purpose of carrying out cancer research with Warburg, which, of course, he had not done at all.)

The reaction of the press was remarkable. Burk informed Warburg that newspaper clippings from all over the country, as well as from Germany, had reached the NCI. Furthermore, Burk had been asked to prepare a report on the energetics of photosynthesis for the US Congress's meeting on the future use of natural resources. Besides Burk, only Melvin Calvin, the Berkeley-based chemist, who was working on the photosynthetic dark reactions (for which he was eventually awarded the Nobel

---

[4]Burk et al. (1951), p. 222.

[5]All quotes in this paragraph: Archive of the BBAW, NL Warburg 174. Burk to Warburg, 2 Feb 1951.

Prize in Chemistry of 1961), and the eminent photochemist Farrington Daniels, had been asked to contribute. Burk explained that this would lead to an enormous proliferation of their findings: every congressman and senator would receive a copy, which amounted to about 10,000 people altogether.[6]

It is worth taking a short glimpse into the scope and style of the newspaper reports on the one-quantum mechanism. The Deutsche Zeitung, for example, featured the headline: *"The chemical miracle plant: Sensational discovery is considered to banish famine."* The author of the article expected that the Warburg–Burk findings would fulfil two dreams of mankind: the eradication of hunger and becoming independent of coal, petrol and wood. Hopes were obviously high: *"The industrial production of a technological-artificial plant is about to be envisaged – an innovation which would revolutionize the world's economy."* The Berlin-based Tagesspiegel trumpeted in a similar manner on 4 March 1951: *"The solar power station of nature: Berlin scientists solve the energetic mystery of the growth of plants."* On 3 May, 1951, Laurence of the New York Times joined in: *"Plant life study yields new data. Science team reports 'cyclic' process in use of sunlight."* In his article, Laurence reported that the discovery of the one-quantum mechanism was the *"crowning achievement of his [Warburg's] life"*, and compared photosynthesis to the pilgrim step, that is, *"three steps forward and two steps back"*. Burk's still bolder plans for the future were also quoted in this article:

> Now that the knowledge is available of the mechanism by which the green plant captures its energy," Dr. Burk said, "the great problem is to find out what substance it is that first picks up the energy in one-quantum lots." Once this is known, it may be possible to devise ways of carrying out photosynthesis by chemical and mechanical means independently of plants. A sun energy factory might then produce a power that would easily replace fuels such as coal, oil, gas and wood. It might also be the basis for synthetic foods.[7]

As a result of all this public enthusiasm, it is not surprising that the NCI was, for the moment, appreciative of Burk and his achievements. And, as Burk wrote to Warburg, his superiors even defended him for not having carried out cancer research: on the strength of this extremely successful sideline of Burk's, Congress should feel even more obliged to support cancer work.[8]

Although the response of photosynthesis researchers was not quite as enthusiastic, the papers were still eagerly received. In April 1951,

---

[6]Cf. Archive of the BBAW, NL Warburg 174. Burk to Warburg, 23 March 1951.

[7]New York Times, Thursday, 3 May 1951.

[8]Archive of the BBAW, NL Warburg 174. Burk to Warburg, 23 March 1951.

Burk wrote to Heiss that Franck was most interested in the large dark combustion phenomenon and had said that, *"if this is definitely established something quite new and unexpected has been discovered, even if I would like to keep an open mind as to the interpretation".*[9] Burk received another tentatively positive reaction from Gaffron, who, according to Burk, had conceded that *"if the new observations must be interpreted as Warburg and you do, they mean of course a revolution in our general concepts. [...] I think the matter is so exciting that I would like to repeat the experiments."* In a similar vein, although very critical of the publication itself, Hill wrote to Emerson, on 28 April 1951:

> *Whittingham and I had a talk about the Burk & Warburg note. [...] You know, unless one had done the B&W experiments oneself it seems impossible to see exactly where the experimental results are from the description. We could not see at the moment how phases can be sufficiently sharply defined in a 1 min alternation of relative or added light & dark. [...] However the Burk Warburg note was very stimulating – and yet did not seem to me to be really sharply focused on any small aspect, like the Papal Bull. And now it leaves the field quite clear for all specific studies. Warburg could do wonders with the purely biochemical parts, of course.*[10]

It is obvious from his response to Hill that Emerson was far less charitable in his evaluation:

> *There isn't much use in trying to discuss the Burk–Warburg 1 minute–1 minute measurements by mail. [...] I don't feel the need of further stimulation such as the new Warburg–Burk paper. I'm still confused as to the proper direction for my own further efforts. I would like to return to some of the problems raised by the Emerson-Lewis measurements at different wave lengths, particularly the sharp drop in efficiency toward the infrared, and the question whether excitation of chlorophyll with "blue" quanta can produce reactions differing in some fundamental way (higher efficiency?) than excitation with "red" quanta. To do this, I would be inclined to go back to single vessel measurements in carbonate mixture, but I feel that Warburg has put upon me a sort of curse, that I may not do this unless I can show beyond doubt that the efficiency measured in carbonate is not inferior to the efficiency in acid phosphate.*[11]

---

[9]This and the following quote were taken from: Archive of the BBAW, NL Warburg 174. Burk to Heiss, 3 April 1951.

[10]Hill to Emerson, 28 April 1951, Robert Emerson Papers, 1923-61, Record Series 15/4/28, Box 1, Folder: Hill, Robin, University of Illinois Archives.

[11]Emerson to Hill, 8 May 1951, Robert Emerson Papers, 1923-61, Record Series 15/4/28, Box 1, Folder: Hill, Robin, University of Illinois Archives.

One could hardly ask for a more explicit formulation of Emerson's sincere wish, by that time, to detach himself from the quantum yield controversy and return to more productive work instead. Yet the "curse" would remain in place for a number of years to come.

2   BURK'S PHOTOSYNTHESIS WARS

In order to get an idea of the undercurrents of the controversy, in particular on Warburg and Burk's side, it seems worth taking an even closer look at how the course of events was reflected in the (large amount of) correspondence between the two. The feeling one gets is that these two actors saw themselves as the victims of an outrageous conspiracy; and that they increasingly started to believe the stories that they had made up about the qualities of their own work and the work of their main opponents. Burk frequently used metaphoric language in his letters; and one might be tempted to think that at least some of these metaphoric expressions were meant to be taken quite literally. Already in his first letter to Warburg, after the latter had returned in 1949 to Germany after his stay in the United States, Burk assured his newly found mentor: *"I am carrying on the photosynthetic war with undiminished vigor."*[12] In his letters to Warburg, Burk repeatedly framed the controversy on the maximum quantum yield as a series of *"battles"* that he had to fight, while the students, whom Warburg and Burk had met in Woods Hole and convinced of the validity of their methods and findings (among them, for example, Martin Klein, Martin Schwartz, Victor Schocken and Mitchell Korzenovsky), were referred to by Burk as their *"converts"* and *"missionaries"*. In a letter of November 1949, Burk wrote to Warburg:

> *And now what about our student converts? They have been kept very busy, in Chicago and Wisconsin, as you can see by the enclosed recent letters I have received by way of report. Emerson spoke in Chicago on Oct. 8 [1949], and requested that Klein and Mitchell be present as "Warburkian" experts, and then a little later Klein himself gave a seminar on our work, and Schwartz then gave one in Wisconsin with results as indicated in the letters, which I enclose copies of, as I am sure that you will find them of interest. How lucky it is that our Woods Hole-trained missionaries are located right in the two main camps of the enemy. They do seem to be stalwart champions to the best of their ability. It looks as if we are going to have just no trouble from Wisconsin. Emerson is evidently still busy trying to pick holes in our work but doing nothing constructive, and apparently nothing for us to worry about. Franck, although no longer on the same ship with Emerson, and*

---

[12]Archive of the BBAW, NL Warburg 174. Burk to Warburg, 2 Nov. 1949.

having relinquished most of his former objections, is still trying to find some new ones, and Gaffron is as hopelessly confused as ever. But none of this adds up to much.[13]

Burk also liked to speak of his *"propaganda work"*. He kept himself extremely busy, driving around the country to spread the *"message"*, as he put it – and there was considerable interest in his presentations. As we explained earlier, most plant physiologists knew very little about the subject; indeed, even most researchers working directly in the field of photosynthesis found the question of the maximum quantum yield obscure. The experimental set-up was complicated and could only be mastered if one was extremely skilled in the technique of manometry, and the uncertainty of the outcome was large. Equally large was the interest by others in the field to see the question resolved; or, at least, have somebody explain to them what was at stake. Burk regularly informed Warburg about visitors to his laboratory, who came to see the incredible values actually being measured. C. Stacy French was among the first: *"French was here all day Wednesday, and his mind was at first back in the year-ago Urbana meeting, but rest assured that he was duly worked on,"* Burk wrote to Warburg in December 1949.[14]

It is unclear how French himself regarded this meeting. However, the slightly distorted way in which Burk perceived events (or, at the very least, reported them to Warburg) can be taken from almost any one of the letters that make up their correspondence, if one either reads between the lines or compares the account with other sources. One example should suffice. In November 1951, Burk told Warburg that he had met, at Stanford, the Dutch photosynthesis researcher Bessel Kok (1918–1979), and had invited the latter to come to Bethesda for the rest of the year. Kok arrived on 19 November 1951, and two weeks later, Burk wrote to Warburg:

> *As you may know, he [Kok] has doubted our work, with some good reason, to a greater extent than anyone else, because he has done so many experiments both before and after Sheffield, and always obtained nothing better than 8, for all practical purposes. He has been in the Spoehr–French laboratory of the Carnegie Institution of Washington at Stanford, California, since May, and they have paid his expenses to come here for a month.*
>
> *It took him two weeks to get here, for enroute he stopped off to see all our dear friends at Urbana, Chicago, Madison and Minnesota, at some of which places he heard that not only were all our experiments very sloppy but that you and I were very deficient in*

---

[13] Archive of the BBAW, NL Warburg 174. Burk to Warburg, 2 Nov. 1949.
[14] Archive of the BBAW, NL Warburg 174. Burk to Warburg, 18 Dec. 1949.

character, lying and cheating being one of our minor vices! In fact I was portrayed as being no scientist but merely a good advertising man, and the gossip picked up about you cannot be put down on paper. Kok had expected to see me literally sweat for four weeks, trying, but never succeeding, to reproduce the 4-quantum figure, so he said. To express it all in another manner, he was the shining knight of these people.

All of this, both the science and the character assay, is entirely changed. In our very first experiment together, with acid media under the old 1949 Bethesda conditions, we produced a figure of 3 1/2, and in the course of the next two weeks we were able to show Kok everything, including good yields with very thin and very thick suspensions, at, above, and below the compensation point, and both in acid media and in your new pH 8.8 carbonate medium. The last results, because of their great simplicity, were naturally the most striking. [...]

At the end of this, Kok said that he had seen everything he had wanted us to show him, and that he would admit to seeing the figure of 3-5 quanta such as he had never really seen in any of his own work. [...] So, we have completely changed over our biggest scientific doubter. It remains to be seen what the effects of his remarks to our other dear friends will be. Perhaps you can make a good guess.[15]

Kok's own reports, however, had a very different tone. Although he did admit to having seen the low quantum yield, he was far from being *"completely changed over"*. Rather, he became thoroughly convinced that Warburg and Burk had misinterpreted their data. After his visit to Bethesda, Kok went on to Chicago and discussed matters with Gaffron and Franck; there he defended the view that, if one took into account the energy of the auxiliary light (which he thought Warburg and Burk had not properly done), this led to efficiency calculations of only about 20 %.[16] Furthermore, in a letter to Burk sent in January 1952, Kok reported how he had discussed the data back at Stanford with *"all the gods from Pacific Grove, Berkeley, etc."*; it was agreed there (in line with the earlier suggestion made by Franck) that the data demonstrated *"that a four and an eight quantum process are observable in one and the same suspension!"* However, which of these processes actually was photosynthesis was a matter of intense debate, Kok wrote. Kok himself preferred to think of photosynthesis as the 8-quantum process, and interpret the 4-quantum

---

[15]Archive of the BBAW, NL Warburg 174. Burk to Warburg, 11 Dec. 1951.

[16]Cf. the letter Emerson to Whittingham, 5 September 1952. Robert Emerson Papers, 1923-61, Record Series 15/4/28, Box 1, Folder: Whittingham, Charles, University of Illinois Archives.

process as respiration suppression.[17] It is highly unlikely that Kok would have spoken to Burk, while he was at Bethesda, in completely different terms, so that one may conclude that either Burk deliberately misled Warburg, in order to take the credit for acquiring a new *"convert"*, or that Burk tended to misunderstand what others said on the subjects of quantum yields, when they did not wholeheartedly approve of his and Warburg's work.

Note, however, that, in the letter to Warburg quoted above, Burk referred to a *"new pH 8.8 carbonate medium"*, which had been demonstrated to Kok, in which Warburg and Burk claimed to have measured the same low quantum yield as in the usual acidic phosphate buffer solution. This effectively protected the new measurements against Emerson's (and his co-workers') unremitting criticism that in a phosphate buffer solution the data were distorted by the carbon dioxide burst. No burst had ever been observed in a carbonate buffer solution; this confounding factor was, therefore, not relevant to Warburg's new data. The question, therefore, was how to explain a maximum quantum yield of 3 in an alkaline medium.[18]

3   THE GATLINBURG CONFERENCE ON PHOTOSYNTHESIS, 1952

One obvious effect of the disagreement between Warburg–Burk on one side and Emerson–Franck–Gaffron et al. on the other was that it increased enormously the frequency with which formal and informal meetings between the various photosynthesis researchers took place. Burk's travels around the country to promote the Warburg–Burk cause have already been mentioned as well as the fact that he eagerly invited people to his laboratory so that they could witness the experiments with their own eyes. Kok was only one of these guests. The desire either to meet personally or to discuss the situation in extended letters also rose dramatically among the major players of the opposing party. One letter by Emerson, arbitrarily selected from the many letters comprising his correspondence on the subject matter, may serve as an example. On 8 May 1951, Emerson wrote to Gaffron:

Dear Hans:

Thanks very much for the time you and Franck took yesterday to talk with us over the phone and tell us the news about Burk, Brackett, etc. We hear from [Sol] Spiegelman that Burk made a convincing impression at Cleveland. It's interesting that his blatant

---

[17] Archive of the BBAW, NL Warburg 174. Kok to Burk, January 1952.
[18] For the pertinent publications, see Warburg et al. (1952) and Warburg (1952).

*self-advertising which offended people in England seems not to
antagonize people in this country.*

*Of course, I'm very sorry that circumstances make it so difficult
for me to join you at Madison on Thursday. I would like very much
to hear what Daniels picked up from Brackett. However, perhaps
we can get together in Chicago, and you can tell us what Daniels
found out. Eugene [Rabinowitch] says he could be in Chicago next
Monday, May 14th. That would suit me very well. [...] Can you
drop me a postal card confirming this plan? If you agree, then I
will show up at your place 10:30 Monday morning.*[19]

Short as it is, this letter alludes to the following events: a telephone
conversation between Emerson, Gaffron, Franck and, presumably, Rabinowitch; a report by Emerson's Urbana colleague Sol Spiegelman, who
had seen Burk at a conference in Cleveland; a meeting scheduled at
Farrington Daniels's laboratory at Madison, at which Daniels would
report about an earlier meeting with the expert in polarography and
spectroscopy Frederick S. Brackett; and a future meeting in Chicago, at
which Gaffron was requested to pass on to Rabinowitch and Emerson the
news received from Daniels. It is probably not exaggerated to see this as
reflecting an intense flow of information within a network of actors.

The common goal of most of these actors was to explain, if at all possible, how Warburg and Burk obtained their implausible data. This was
the main reason why researchers either wanted to go and look at Burk's
experiments in Bethesda (Warburg's experiments in Dahlem were too far
off for a short visit) or wished to meet independently, in order to discuss
experimental methods, data and alternative interpretations. Frequently,
both approaches were combined: for example, Kok, as mentioned earlier,
went on to Chicago to discuss his experiences at Bethesda with Franck
and Gaffron. In a similar vein, also the plant physiologist Allan H. Brown
visited Burk in Bethesda; and although he was still unconvinced of the
validity of Burk's data and his interpretations, Brown turned to Emerson
afterwards with the following inquiry:

*I should like to ask you again about the extent to which you have
studied the alleged "accelerated combustion" phenomena. [...] It
seems that the situation is in this case different from that of the
four quanta dispute. In the earlier controversy Warburg's results
could be repeated if one designed the same inherent errors into
the experiment, but for the "accelerated combustion" I believe no
such duplication has been obtained. Is my interpretation correct
that you have looked for the effect and not found it? In discussions*

---

[19]Emerson to Gaffron, 8 May 1951, Robert Emerson Papers, 1923-61, Record Series
15/4/28, Box 1, Folder: Gaffron, Hans, University of Illinois Archives.

*with Burk and people of that school it is not very effective to claim
that the effect is not observed. Burk counters with the argument
that the conditions were not right.*[20]

The latter remark, of course, hit the nail on the head. The quantum
yield experiments had shown themselves to be so complicated that one
had truly to master the methods if one were to obtain any useful data
at all. Warburg and Burk, like everybody else, were fully aware of the
situation and did not hesitate to capitalize on it. And while Emerson, in
principle, knew what he had to do, in order to undermine the most recent
Warburg–Burk approach – the "accelerated combustion phenomenon", as
Brown called it –, he had not yet succeeded in evaluating it. As he replied
to Brown, Emerson's major criticism of Warburg and Burk's one-minute
interval measurements was the following:

*They [Warburg and Burk] have no proper basis for justifying the
baseline rate of exchange, which would be respiration if they alternated measured light with darkness, but which is an unknown
mixture of respiration and photosynthesis in their experiments with
unmeasured auxiliary light. The effect of the measured light can
only be calculated from some assumed background rate whether or
not auxiliary light is used, and I doubt that the provisions they
have made for establishing the background rate in their prolonged
one-minute-light, one-minute-dark experiments can be regarded as
dependable.*[21]

Although this was a serious point of concern, Emerson as well as
Brown knew that this problem could not possibly be resolved at the
moment, neither by Burk nor by Emerson, and surely not through using
manometric methods. This, incidentally, was one of the reasons for the
fact that Brown was no longer in favor of manometry. At the time, Brown
was writing a review of photosynthesis research with Albert Frenkel. In
this article, Brown and Frenkel (1953) strongly suggested that, in view
of the clear limitations of manometry, other methods should be used
to settle the debate, preferably physical techniques, such as infra-red
spectrometry, polarography, mass spectrometry and others.[22] Emerson,
however, never lost his faith in manometry; he continuously strove to

---

[20]Brown to Emerson, 25 May 1952, Robert Emerson Papers, 1923-61, Record Series
15/4/28, Box 1, Folder: Brown, Allan, University of Illinois Archives. "Accelerated
combustion" refers here to the high oxygen consumption that Warburg and Burk
claimed to have found, which was thought to be used for respiratory purposes (that
is, for the "combustion" of carbohydrates).

[21]Emerson to Brown, 28 May 1952, Robert Emerson Papers, 1923-61, Record Series
15/4/28, Box 1, Folder: Brown, Allan, University of Illinois Archives.

[22]See Brown & Frenkel (1953), p. 426.

improve the technique, for example, by using double differential manometers, which were far more precise than the usual single ones. Also the light sources and the other pieces of the set-up were subjected to continuous re-evaluation. Thus, Emerson wrote to Lewis in June 1952 and asked for the latter's laboratory notebooks of the work they had done on quantum yield of oxygen evolution around 1940. At the time, Emerson was trying to set up an improved monochromator, and thought that Lewis's notes would be very helpful. He was well aware that to Lewis this request must have sounded rather strange:

> *It must sound funny to you, who have wrestled with such diverse problems since our ways parted, to hear that I am still struggling with the same things which baffled us twelve or thirteen years ago. The efficiency of photosynthesis is a stubborn problem, and it seems one can only hope to make progress by making some fairly fundamental improvements in technique. Ever since the Palo Alto days, I've been unable to put anything like the consecutive effort into the work, which you and I achieved for those three years.*[23]

In this summer of 1952, preparations got underway for a large conference on photosynthesis that would take place in Gatlinburg, Tennessee, at the end of October, supported by the National Science Foundation, the Office of Naval Research and the Atomic Energy Commission.[24] On 1 July, 1952, Emerson received a letter from Hendricks inviting him to participate in this conference, *"for the purpose of examining those aspects of the subject which appear to be limiting further understanding"*.[25] The format was intended to encourage free discussion among the participants: No formal papers were scheduled, but sessions of full half days were reserved for every theme, with an additional, uncommitted day at the end of the conference. An introductory speaker would, at the beginning of each session, briefly review the subject matter; while immediately afterwards the floor would be given to anyone in the audience: *"Everyone should be prepared with slides and illustrative material on whatever is felt to be pertinent to the subject,"* Hendricks pointed out in his letter.

Emerson was feeling pretty desperate when he received the invitation. As he wrote to Charles Whittingham on 5 September, 1952, for the greater part of the year he had been trying to free himself from Warburg's shadow, leaving the quantum yield question aside and following

---

[23] Emerson to Lewis on 19 Juni 1952, Robert Emerson Papers, 1923-61, Record Series 15/4/28, Box 1, Folder: Lewis, Charlton. University of Illinois Archives.

[24] A short summary of the conference's discussions is provided in Hendricks (1953).

[25] This and the following quote: Hendricks to Emerson, 1 July 1952, Robert Emerson Papers, 1923-61, Record Series 15/4/28, Box 1, Folder: Gatlinburg Conference, University of Illinois Archives.

up some other lines of research, among other things, a thorough study of the carbon dioxide burst and its relationship to temperature and other variables. Emerson was aware that these studies would not contribute to resolving the controversy, yet, as he wrote with some exasperation: *"I feel I cannot always submit to being led around by the nose by that deceitful old poker player, and must sometimes test out one or two of my own ideas."*[26] However, one full session was being reserved for the quantum yield question at the Gatlinburg conference, and Emerson knew that, because of Warburg's latest publications, the audience would expect much of his contribution:

> *Warburg's new papers, reporting high efficiencies in carbonate mixtures, etc., have excited a good deal of interest. I've tried to give them the brush-off, saying that he has not established the dark-rate on the basis of which he calculates light action, and looking always for the weak spot which I feel sure is there, concealed as cleverly as possible by the crafty old poker player. But our analysis of the errors inherent in Warburg and Burk's 2-vessel technique, adequate though it was for the refutation of their claims up to 1950 or so, is of no help in elucidating the meaning of the one-vessel measurements in carbonate buffer [solution].*
>
> *Shimpe [Nishimura] assures me that at Gatlinburg, everyone will want to know what, if anything, is wrong with the carbonate mixture single-vessel quantum yield measurements. He thinks the trouble comes from Warburg's (obviously incorrect) assumption that there is no significant physical lag, but neither Shimpe nor I can see how this could produce the high efficiencies.*
>
> *Ever since last spring, Shimpe has been maturing in his mind a plan to test the errors in Warburg's single-vessel experiments, and now I have let him tear down my experimental set-up, build one simulating Warburg's, and see what he can find. He's trying to get some answers before he goes to California for his vacation. He wants to give me some ammunition to take to Gatlinburg. I'm pessimistic about his chances of settling anything in a short time. I remember how long it took us to find out that in the two-vessel method the only significant source of error was difference in physical lag in the two vessels. But you never can tell what Shimpe will hit upon.*[27]

While Emerson was obviously tired of the whole affair, Burk, who had also been invited to Gatlinburg, was enthusiastic. Warburg declined his

[26] Emerson to Whittingham, 5 Sept. 1952, Robert Emerson Papers, 1923-61, Record Series 15/4/28, Box 1, Folder: Whittingham, Charles, University of Illinois Archives.

[27] Emerson to Whittingham, 5 Sept. 1952, Robert Emerson Papers, 1923-61, Record Series 15/4/28, Box 1, Folder: Whittingham, Charles, University of Illinois Archives.

invitation, although he did send Burk some slides with new data to use in the discussion. Burk made diligent preparations, since he did not expect the *"game"* to be easy. As he wrote to Warburg on 28 August 1952: *"I too agree that the cold war on the quantum yield is in fact getting more intense and may soon develop into a hot one, abroad as well as here."*[28] Warburg was obviously concerned about the outcome (perhaps he recalled the Sheffield meeting of 1950, where Burk did not make a very favorable impression upon the audience) and raised the possibility that Burk should also turn down the invitation. However, Burk had sufficient confidence in himself and thought it would be unwise not to go: *"Because if none of us shows up there people will surely get, or maliciously create, the impression that we have 'lost heart' or become afraid.'*[29] Warburg's alternative suggestion was to find again, as in Urbana 1948, an impartial judge to pass an authoritative sentence after having heard the arguments; but this was countered by Burk with the objection that he could not think of anybody who would fit the role. Warburg's concerns that the other side's preparations would be at least as thorough as Burk's were not unfounded. On 27 October 1952, Burk wrote to Warburg, just before he set off for Tennessee:

> A week ago, I am reliably told, Gaffron telephoned here to [Frederick S.] Brackett and arranged for the extra Saturday session on the quantum requirement, in which Brackett was asked to take the role of ringleader, and [Sterling] Hendricks has warned me: "They are all against you." But we think we are ready for them, and I enclose one of the slides of data which shows not only the 1-quantum measurements in alkaline solution (bottom part of the table) but also how the rate of shaking (if inadequate) can affect the quantum yield (utilization of light) even though the manometric gas equilibration is perfect, as shown by identical rates of respiration at both rates of shaking (150 and 210).[30]

Thus, at the Gatlinburg conference there was to be not one but two sessions on the question of quantum requirements; and one can assume that this was done with the hope of settling the issue once and for all. How the meeting proceeded can be taken both from Burk's elaborate and highly detailed letter to Warburg and from a short review written by Hendricks (1953) for Science. By all accounts, it was an extremely lively meeting, with discussions lasting each day from early morning till late at night; and the sessions on quantum yields were among the liveliest. The first session, Burk reported to Warburg, was dominated by

---

[28] Archive of the BBAW, NL Warburg 174. Burk to Warburg, 28 Aug. 1952.

[29] Archive of the BBAW, NL Warburg 174. Burk to Warburg, 12 Sept. 1952.

[30] Archive of the BBAW, NL Warburg 174. Burk to Warburg, 27 Oct. 1952.

"the Old Guard", or, as Burk alternatively put it, the *"Murderers' Row"*, which comprised *"Brackett, Gaffron, Daniels, Arnold, Emerson, Brown, French, and Franck, etc."* Burk continued in his report:

> *[They got up one after the other and] beat unmercifully, and surely unscientifically, at both the 4- and the 1-quantum. The attack was far worse than at Sheffield and carefully timed and planned before- hand, to create the impression among the rest of the audience that both the 4- and the 1-quantum values were impossible, absurd and easy to explain. During all this while I didn't say anything but just sat looking unconcerned, smoking one cigar after another, while the situation seemingly got blacker and blacker.*[31]

Things were not looking good for Burk's camp. Brackett presented the data that he had obtained using polarographic methods, which showed that the minimum quantum requirement was 6–10 per molecule of oxy- gen. Brown reported that mass spectroscopy gave no evidence of a sub- stantial consumption of oxygen in the dark phase, as would be expected with the one-quantum mechanism. Gaffron demonstrated that photosyn- thesis could be initiated without any trace of oxygen, which is, without the probability of back reactions occurring such as those described in the one-quantum mechanism. According to Burk, Daniels presented, *"with obvious facetiousness (and with some amusement)"*, the results obtained by Burk's student converts in Daniels's laboratory, one of which had arrived at values of around 9, while the other had *"agreed on the average with those of Warburg and Burk but individually varied from 3 to 14, in such manner that no confidence could be placed in them"*.[32] Finally, Emerson reported that he had been unable to find any difference in outcome between the old and new carbonate mixtures, both of which generally gave quantum requirement of 9. Emerson also made it very clear that, in view of the wealth of data that contradicted the high Warburgian yield, it was no longer Emerson's responsibility to explain why he did not get the same results as Warburg and Burk, but that it was now up to Warburg and Burk to examine their experiments to find out why they did not get the same results as everyone else.[33] Emerson most probably made this remark in response to Burk's attitude at this session. As Brown had foreseen in his letter to Emerson (quoted above), Burk refused to take any notice of other people's measurements, unless they had demonstrated manometrically that they had been able to get a quantum requirement of 4 under conditions as Warburg and Burk had recently specified them.

---

[31] Archive of the BBAW, NL Warburg 174. Burk to Warburg, 13 Nov. 1952.

[32] All quotes: Archive of the BBAW, NL Warburg 174. Burk to Warburg, 13 Nov. 1952.

[33] Archive of the BBAW, NL Warburg 819. Arthur Schade to Warburg, 5 Dec. 1952.

Failures to do so were regarded by Burk as evidence of nothing but the researcher's incompetence.

The discussion was resumed on the last day of the conference, in a session chaired by French. On this occasion, Franck took the opportunity to talk for nearly one hour, explaining in detail the principles underlying the energy accumulation in photosynthesis. This talk made an enormous impression upon the audience. Emerson wrote to Franck afterwards that he had never before heard Franck give so clear an exposition of the energy losses and energy requirement involved in photosynthesis.[34] Even Burk admitted to Warburg that these thermodynamical considerations seemed to be, at present, the most potent objection to the four- and one-quantum theory: *"Franck looks at this slide [on which the energy balance was written in detail], and then sings a chorus, in which a great number join, that Burk and Warburg are tampering with not only the first but the second law of thermodynamics, in short, denying God himself."*[35]

In addition to that, Franck also made a new attempt to reconcile the Warburg–Burk data with the data obtained by other groups, along the same lines as earlier (thereby suggesting that Warburg and Burk had, in actual fact, measured the yield of a different photochemical process). This was endorsed by Kok, who was the next to speak and who pointed out that he had witnessed the low quantum requirement being reached only under conditions where respiration was likely to interfere substantially with photosynthesis (compare this with Burk's description of Kok's attitude after his visit to Bethesda). Finally, it was Burk's turn to talk, as he wrote to Warburg:

> *I then got up and spoke for the rest of the session, and had the last word, so to speak, or at least the next to the last word, since there was nearly a half hour of discussion after I got through. [...] My general attitude was that here were the data, and our conclusions, but anybody who wished to believe otherwise, for the next five or ten years at least, could do so and see where such other beliefs might lead him.*

The general impression one gets from Burk's letter is that he had finally lost all sense of reality. Burk continuously divided people into two camps: the supporters of his and Warburg's "cause" on the one side; the opponents on the other. Burk again emphasized that at Gatlinburg he had also managed to *"get a number of new converts to our side"*, while he

---

[34]Emerson to Franck, 13 Nov. 1952, Robert Emerson Papers, 1923-61, Record Series 15/4/28, Box 1, Folder: Franck, James, University of Illinois Archives.

[35]This and the following quotes by Burk: Archive of the BBAW, NL Warburg 174. Burk to Warburg, 13 Nov. 1952.

frowned at *"a middle group of fence-sitters, like Sterling Hendricks, who still mainly point their heads in the direction of the other side and their tails to ours"*; to which Burk added: *"In any dictionary of the American language, such people are known as mugwumps."* Obviously, Burk found this refusal to take a stand completely unacceptable.

It seems that people at the conference, notably Hill, had the impression that Burk was on a slippery slope and that it would be wise if he detached himself from Warburg before it was too late – the sooner, the better. Burk reported also these details to his master:

> *Well, in addition to science, there were all kinds of personalia and various "kind" people like Robin Hill and Kok and others advised me to drop any further work on the quantum yield or even photosynthesis in general before I lost my scientific reputation altogether! That you should lose yours was perhaps of lesser moment to them, than that such a nice and kind person as myself should do so!!! And so the crocodile tears rolled on, from some people. On the other hand, after the final meeting, Calvin, who I am sure is no great believer in the 4- and 1-quantum, told my wife, "You tell your husband to keep on fighting."*

> *Robin Hill, who is the only person to flatly refuse to contribute to the festschrift [in honour of Warburg's seventieth birthday], spoke very frankly to me and it is quite obvious that he shares the Cambridge views about you personally, and he said to me quite frankly that in his opinion you were a "rogue" and did not mind who knew it. He also stated to me that he had the highest opinion of Emerson personally and scientifically, and it is obvious that they are great friends [. . .]. Hill said that you have been unforgivably rude to not only [David] Keilin but various others at Cambridge. I asked him whether it was more important to be rude or actually scientifically wrong and stupid, and he said frankly that he preferred to be stupid rather than rude – a matter of taste in any event.*[36]

The interesting point here, however, is that, although the majority of photosynthesis researchers by then believed that Burk and Warburg were using dirty rhetorical tricks and that they were behaving in an utterly unacceptable manner – when it came to dealing with factual criticism and divergent points of view, this did not change the fact that the maximum value of the quantum yield of photosynthesis was still unknown. So, for example, even though Hill was thoroughly disgusted with Warburg and Burk's conduct, this did not prevent him from paying a visit to Burk's laboratory shortly after the Gatlinburg conference, in order to see the disputed results with his own eyes and to discuss

---

[36]Archive of the BBAW, NL Warburg 174. Burk to Warburg, 13 Nov. 1952.

photosynthetic matters with Burk. Indeed, Hill had tried, together with Whittingham, to reproduce the Warburg–Burk values; the attempt had failed, but Hill wished to try it again and therefore needed to go over some of the experimental details, as Burk proudly explained to Warburg: *"He [Hill] agreed that just plain negative results, without understanding, mean nothing, and he agreed that Brown's results wouldn't mean anything until Brown first repeated our results and could then show, by the mass spectrograph, if anything were wrong with them".*[37]

In truth, Hill was very interested in how respiratory back reactions might interfere with photosynthesis and its quantum yield; and this interest was clearly strong enough for him to try and find out from Burk as much as possible about the measurements in question – even though, on a personal level, Hill would have preferred to talk to somebody else. The new measurements taken in a carbonate buffer solution really had reintroduced a new sense of uncertainty. While the carbon dioxide burst had undermined all the measurements taken in an acidic medium, Warburg and Burk now seemed to be able to measure low quantum yields in carbonate-bicarbonate buffer. The fact that Emerson claimed to be unable to reproduce the data was not received as a satisfactory counter argument, and justifiably so. Negative results – in this case, the failure to replicate a certain experimental finding – were not a fatal blow, particularly when the experiments required such delicate handling, as quantum yield measurements did. Whittingham succinctly summarized the situation, as he and Hill saw it, in a letter to Emerson in March 1953:

> *The question arises – supposing W's observations were genuine – what possible explanation is there? One postulates a further carboxylation process in the stronger buffer. One then tries to find evidence for or against that point of view. This we think is found lacking [...]. The isolated fact that W. did or did not get what he claims is of little interest without reference as to how it affects one's preconceived notions. So we think!*[38]

Despite the prevailing skepticism among photosynthesis researchers, Burk received the 1952 Hillebrand Prize of the Chemical Society of Washington (the local American Chemical Society Chapter for the Washington, DC area) *"for the experimental discovery of a photosynthetic energy cycle of high quantum efficiency, with demonstration of the applicability of the Einstein law of photochemical equivalence".*[39] Emerson was well

---

[37] Archive of the BBAW, NL Warburg 174. Burk to Warburg, 13 Dec. 1952.

[38] Whittingham to Emerson, 2 March 1953, Robert Emerson Papers, 1923-61, Record Series 15/4/28, Box 1, Folder: Whittingham, Charles, University of Illinois Archives.

[39] Archive of the BBAW, NL Warburg 174 Burk to Warburg, 17 Jan. 1953.

aware that, because of Warburg's new data in carbonate-bicarbonate buffer, he now had to defend his position once again; and he was also aware that he and his colleagues were engaged in battle with a powerful enemy, in both scientific and rhetorical terms. After the conference, Emerson wrote to Franck:

> *This letter is primarily to express to you my appreciation of your presence among those of us who are working in the field of photosynthesis. You have sometimes been distressed because you felt your contribution was not as great as you would like to make it. But as I listened to you at Gatlinburg I felt, more than I ever did before, the value of the leadership which you have brought to the field. Your presence among us was an incentive to all of us to make our own contributions on the highest possible plane. There are not many people who could provide this sort of inspiration, and you are the only one in the photosynthesis group. (I must say that I think Hill may come in time to exert a similar quality of leadership, though in quite a different way, because he lacks your background in physics and photochemistry.) I need not mention to you the names of the other men who would be dominant figures in the photosynthesis group if you were not among us, but their names and faces flitted through my mind as I listened to the talks in Gatlinburg, and I thought how glad I was that you were with us.*[40]

4 EMERSON STRIKES BACK

Even though Emerson was weary of the maximum quantum yield question, after the Gatlinburg meeting of 1952 he returned to working relentlessly towards obtaining results that would validate his own point of view and refute the Warburg–Burk picture of photosynthesis. In January 1954, Emerson apologized to Hill for having failed to keep in touch with him – the reason being, Emerson explained, that he had slowly started to obtain some useful experimental results:

> *It was a matter of achieving a combination of very improbable states, simultaneously. Enough light energy, necessary optical parts, cathetometer telescopes, Mrs. Chalmers getting enough experience in taking readings, etc., etc. We are beginning to find out how Warburg and Burk can get some of the results they claim. After several years of deeply disappointing and frustrating failures, when I suddenly began to get some hopeful results, I just decided to neglect everything else. Even so, the work seems to move at a*

---

[40] Emerson to Franck, 13 Nov. 1952, Robert Emerson Papers, 1923-61, Record Series 15/4/28, Box 1, Folder: Franck, James, University of Illinois Archives.

snail's pace. The cellular processes are terribly intricate, that is to say, the cells have so great a capacity for adjustment that no single experiment is ever by itself conclusive. Each day's work seems to require that 10 more days be spent to clear up the new doubts raised. But at least I am working on the cells and their photosynthesis, and not on the apparatus![41]

Emerson spent much of 1954 with Ruth Chalmers, a long-standing co-worker and expert in algae culturing, on a sabbatical leave in George E. Briggs's laboratory at the University of Cambridge. There Emerson found the necessary peace and freedom to focus on the required experimental work and on writing it up. The result was a lengthy manuscript, co-authored with Chalmers, which was completed in May 1955. Emerson submitted the paper to the journal Plant Physiology and, at the same time, sent out copies to a number of colleagues, whom he asked for comments. In the accompanying letter to Daniels, Emerson explained why the text had grown so much in length:

I feel apologetic about the length of the manuscript, but it is a good deal shorter than the sum total of the papers Warburg and Burk have published during the time we spent doing this work. It was my hope that I could write something which would provide readers with a basis for forming an independent opinion on the significance of the Warburg–Burk contributions, and save them the embarrassment of basing their opinions on the personal prestige of the authors. In my efforts to achieve this, I'm afraid, I let the paper become much too long![42]

Franck was the next to receive a copy of the text, and from him, Emerson requested a very specific type of comment:

I would like very much to know whether you think the standpoint from which it is written is a useful one, and also whether you think I have suppressed contentious remarks about Warburg and Burk. I wish I could make my writing as free of prickly statements as yours is. [. . .] I'm sorry that it is so long. Maybe I'm beating a dead horse?[43]

The manuscript succeeded in making a major impression, as one can take from a letter Emerson wrote to Whittingham shortly thereafter:

---

[41] Cambridge University Library, Ms. Add. 9267/J.54, Emerson to Hill, 4 Jan. 1954.

[42] Emerson to Daniels, 16 June 1955, Robert Emerson Papers, 1923-61, Record Series 15/4/28, Box 1, Folder: Daniels, Farrington, University of Illinois Archives.

[43] Emerson to Franck, 17 June 1955, Robert Emerson Papers, 1923-61, Record Series 15/4/28, Box 1, Folder: Franck, James, University of Illinois Archives.

"I have a long letter from Gaffron with his comments, and have spoken with Franck on the telephone about it. Gaffron tells me that for the first time Franck begins to understand my objections to the experimental work of Warburg and Burk!"[44] On 28 July, 1955, the paper was accepted for publication, although the journal's editor, David Goddard, strongly recommended that either the material should be reorganized or that it be divided into two papers. However, in the end it remained in one piece, published, in November of the same year, as Emerson & Chalmers (1955).

The paper took up no less than twenty-six pages of the journal, and revisited all the major criticisms directed at Warburg's experiments and clarified the diverging points of view. The main purpose of the paper was, as Emerson and Chalmers emphasized, to consider the value of the methods with which photosynthetic efficiencies of 70 % or even higher had been found. Their two primary concerns in doing so was: first, to establish the existence or non-existence of a time lag between the changes of gas pressure inside the cell and the observable changes in the manometer readings; and, second, to establish the potential influence of transient gas exchanges on the calculations of photosynthetic efficiency. Emerson and Chalmers gave a detailed evaluation of the methods involved, and drew the following conclusions:

(i) Even under the conditions chosen by Warburg and Burk the influence of time lag was appreciable, primarily due to diffusion effects between liquid and gas space.

(ii) Apparent absence of time lag was due to the obscuring effect of compensatory processes in the vessel.

If these factors were not taken into consideration, when interpreting the manometrically obtained quantum yield data, the efficiency calculations would be affected in a complicated, and surely significant, manner. (See Figure IV.2 for a representation of Emerson and Chalmer's data.)

In order to establish these claims, Emerson & Chalmers (1955) had striven to duplicate exactly the Warburg–Burk experimental set-up, even though they found it inadequate in many respects. They diverged from this set-up in only one detail, namely, in their choice of manometer. In explaining their reasons for this, Emerson and Chalmers drew attention to the fact that, if they had used Warburg's two-vessel method, then they would have needed to take three manometer readings at the same time while the manometer was being vigorously shaken. *"Even with the aid of a hand lens, a precision of ± 0.5 mm is the utmost that can be expected,"*

---

[44]Emerson to Whittingham, 25 June 1955, Robert Emerson Papers, 1923-61, Record Series 15/4/28, Box 1, Folder: Whittingham, Charles, University of Illinois Archives.

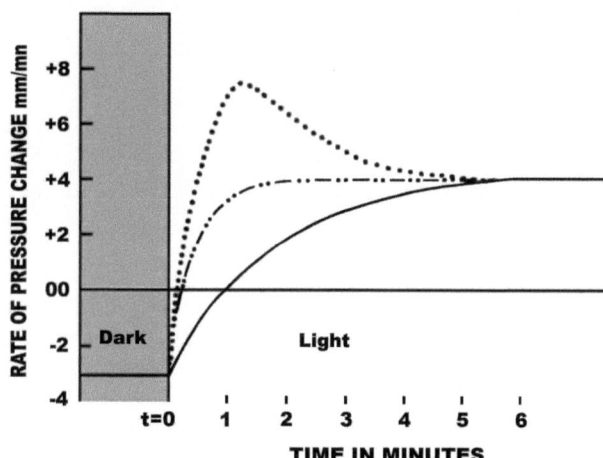

Figure IV.2: A diagram of gas exchange during a dark to light transition, as published by Emerson and Chalmers (1955). The top curve (dots) shows the phenomenon that Emerson and co-workers described for cells suspended in acid phosphate medium. The middle curve (dashes) shows what Warburg and co-workers observed for cells in acid culture medium. The solid line represents the type of transition observed by Emerson and Lewis for cells suspended in carbonate-bicarbonate buffer. Thus, if the acid culture (or phosphate) medium is used, and if the initial "gas burst" (due to CO_2 burst) is included, one will obtain erroneous higher quantum yields of oxygen evolution than in carbonate-bicarbonate buffer.

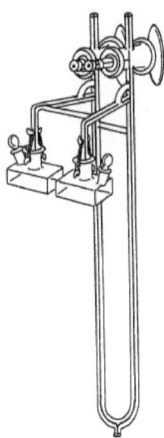

Figure IV.3: The differential manometer used by Emerson and Chalmers: *"One vessel is used as a compensating vessel with suspending fluid but no cells. The other vessel is for the experimental material. For two-vessel measurements, a second manometer is required, with a pair of vessels larger than the pair shown here."* The advantage of this type of manometer is that it is a closed system that requires no additional barometer vessel and no pinchcock adjustment for constant volume. (Reproduced from Emerson & Chalmers (1955), p. 507.)

Emerson and Chalmers maintained; as Warburg's findings were often taken from pressure changes of 3 mm, the resulting range of uncertainty would have amounted to about 30 %![45] *"Greater precision is attainable,"* Emerson and Chalmers explained, *"by reading the manometers with a cathetometer (horizontal telemicroscope with cross-hairs and screw adjustment for height, and scale divided into hundredths of a mm), but the constant-volume type of manometer [which Warburg used] does not lend itself to reading by cathetometer".* (See Figure IV.4 for a photograph of Emerson's cathetometer.) Therefore, in contrast to Warburg's protocol, the authors used differential manometers, which would enable them to

---

[45] It is interesting to see that, besides the paper he had written with Nishimura and Whittingham in 1951, when discussing these potential inaccuracies, Emerson also cited the work carried out in the laboratory of the German plant physiologist André Pirson, namely Pirson, Krollpfeiffer & Schaefer (1953). Pirson was one of the few experts working in Germany at the time who was highly critical of Warburg's claims. See Pirson (1994) for an autobiographical review.

reduce reading errors to a precision of $\pm$ 0.03 mm. (See Figure IV.3 for an illustration.) With the help of these instruments, Emerson & Chalmers (1955) demonstrated that, under the conditions chosen by Warburg and using his methods of calculation, enormously high quantum yields could be reached, although they did not reflect the true quantum yield of photosynthesis. The authors painstakingly spelled out the details of their set-up, mentioning every possible source of error in the experiments (and, at the same time, demonstrating that their errors were much smaller than the ones implied in Warburg and Burk's experiments); they were able to explain how the changes Warburg made to his set-up altered some of the details of his data; they demonstrated that a diffusion lag was a factor that, even under the conditions chosen by Warburg, influenced the outcome of the experiments in relevant ways (although Warburg constantly claimed otherwise); and they concluded that, on every account, the application of the two-vessel method, constantly used by Warburg and his co-workers, was inappropriate for determining transient metabolic rates. This is how Emerson & Chalmers (1955) formulated the essence of the paper:

> *This discussion of the interrelations of diffusion lag and transitional rates of gas exchange leads inevitably to the conclusion that measurements of the efficiency of photosynthesis are significant only when they are based upon steady metabolic rates. The results we have reported here support the conclusion reached earlier by a number of other investigators, that a quantum requirement of about eight per molecule of oxygen produced represents the highest efficiency that can be sustained by the evidence (equivalent to about 30% in red light). The claims put forward by Warburg and co-workers that from one to four quanta suffice per molecule of oxygen produced, appear to be founded upon experimental methods which cannot be counted upon to give results which are numerically correct, and the results, whether correct or not, cannot be regarded as an appropriate basis for calculating the efficiency of photosynthesis.*[46]

As a postscript to this, it should be mentioned that Warburg had, in the meantime, turned to Samuel D. Cornell (1915–2010), the Executive Officer of the National Academy of Sciences (NAS) of the United States. In his letter, dated 25 July 1955, Warburg had expressed his concern that American scientists, notwithstanding the fact that these achievements had completely changed the general understanding of photosynthesis, were continuously contesting several important developments in the field of photosynthesis research, achieved in his laboratory. Warburg reminded

---

[46]Emerson & Chalmers (1955), p. 528.

Cornell of the fact that *"in the days of Pasteur, whose discoveries were often contested in a similar way, the French Academy of Sciences settled the disputes by naming commissions to look at and to check the disputed experiments"*.[47] He therefore appealed to Cornell to send such a commission to Berlin-Dahlem, where Warburg had recently set-up a special laboratory for demonstration purposes. Cornell forwarded this letter to Calvin, Daniels, Emerson, Franck, Goddard and Hendricks, as the experts among the Academy's members, with a request for suggestions as to how the Academy should respond.

The answers Cornell received were clear and unanimous. Emerson wrote that he did not see how sending a delegation to Berlin would serve any good purpose. He reminded Cornell that, for a long time, a number of courteous efforts had been made to draw Warburg's attention to errors that were inherent in his measurements, but none of these had elicited from Warburg any sign of willingness to re-examine his work. *"Rather, he has shown an arrogance in overlooking [his critics'] work and writings, which is unbecoming to his profession. Sometimes he has evaded criticism by cunning and specious arguments,"* Emerson wrote. A visit by a delegation of the Academy, Emerson believed, would not help to clarify the question, *"but would probably be made the basis of a new emphasis upon his prestige, a circumstance which is without direct bearing upon the problems of photosynthesis with which we are concerned"*.[48]

Franck's response to Cornell was that Warburg's letter placed him in an awkward position: if Warburg received a negative answer, he was likely to use this as an argument for the fact that his opponents shunned the objective testing of results. Yet Franck could still not agree to setting up such a committee. First, he underlined that it was impossible to settle the dispute this way: *"Apparently Warburg supposes that it is enough to demonstrate a few examples of manometric measurements from which data may be calculated which support his views. If most of the data do not give the desired results he will explain as he has done often that it is only necessary that some of the data fit because one cannot expect that the biological material is always present in perfect conditions."* However, the main reason that Franck advised against sending a delegation was more fundamental and was based on his understanding as to how science should be made to work:

> I believe that it is not the task of our academy to sit in judgment
> about scientific differences of opinions. As usual a great part of this

---

[47] A copy of Warburg's letter of 25 July 1955 is preserved in: Franck, James. Papers, [Box 10, Folder 1], Special Collections Research Center, University of Chicago Library.

[48] Emerson to Cornell, 10 Aug. 1955. Franck, James. Papers, [Box 10, Folder 1], Special Collections Research Center, University of Chicago Library.

struggle refers not simply to a set of somewhat involved routine measurements but mainly to their interpretation.

Obviously, every scientist has the right to his own opinions but he has the duty to weigh the evidence and the opinions of others and to discard them only after due consideration. Warburg's method to call everyone who disagrees with him incompetent does not offer a practical solution. The scientist has, furthermore, the duty to read the literature to see whether his opinions are inconsistent with results gained in indirectly related fields. Again, Warburg's regards it as unnecessary to do so because as one of his co-workers announced in a meeting the modern literature is not worth reading and only results coming out of Warburg's laboratory amount to anything. If against expectation Warburg's harsh judgment should be correct then that will have to be shown by careful studies and experimentation and not by a quick judgment of a committee based on observations of a few experiments. [...]

[T]he decision what is right and what is wrong should be left to the normal process of the development of science which is after all, a very efficient way to weed out errors even if the processes might not be as quick. After studying the problem carefully for years, I am convinced that the right is not on Warburg's side. Even a scientist as outstanding as Warburg can be occasionally wrong and that is to my regret this time the case in his photosynthetic studies of the last years.[49]

This was also Melvin Calvin's opinion: the question whether or not an individual's results and interpretations were accepted by others should be determined in the usual way, Calvin wrote to Cornell, *"namely, by the willingness and interest of the scientific world in the form of the collection of individual scientists to undertake to test the results and theories proposed by Prof. Warburg"*.[50] Finally, Farrington Daniels informed Emerson that he had discussed the subject in informal talks at a conference in Geneva, Switzerland, with Eugene Rabinowitch, Calvin and the physiologist Detlev W. Bronk (1897–1975), who was at the time President of the Academy. All four of them had agreed that *"it would be a bad precedent for the US National Academy of Science to appoint a committee when scientists disagree. There would be no end of such committees."* To this more official decision, Daniels added in his letter to Emerson: *"Personally, I do not feel that Warburg is entitled to any more consideration than was given to him by you and your laboratory a few*

---

[49] Franck to Cornell, 15 Aug. 1955. Franck, James. Papers, [Box 10, Folder 1], Special Collections Research Center, University of Chicago Library.

[50] Calvin to Cornell, 26 Aug. 1955. Franck, James. Papers, [Box 10, Folder 1], Special Collections Research Center, University of Chicago Library.

years ago. Warburg's letter is really quite astounding. The less attention we pay to it, the better."[51]

Figure IV.4: Emerson's cathetometers, which are the two tall cylindrical objects in the foreground; these were used by Emerson (and then by Govindjee and his group at Urbana) to measure pressure changes within hundredths of a millimeter change. In this photo, Paul Jursinic (who received his PhD in Biophysics under Govindjee in 1977) is holding the lamp assembly that Emerson used to give the second illumination when he discovered the Emerson Enhancement Effect. (The photograph was taken by Govindjee in 1975.)

---

[51]Daniels to Emerson, 26 Aug. 1955, Robert Emerson Papers, 1923-61, Record Series 15/4/28, Box 1, Folder: Daniels, Farrington, University of Illinois Archives.

Chapter V

THE AFTERMATH

1   THE ENHANCEMENT EFFECT

After the paper by Emerson and Chalmers of 1955, most people in the field had become convinced that the number of 8 to 10 quanta as a minimum requirement for the evolution of one oxygen molecule was at least approximately the accurate one; while any further (and, perhaps, a more definitive) resolution of the question had to wait for the development of new methods. A general saturation point had been reached and many participants felt that the problem had been discussed for far too many years and in far too much depth – almost *ad nauseam*. This was reflected, for example, in the fact that the theme of the maximum quantum yield of photosynthesis was deliberately excluded from the second Gatlinburg conference on photosynthesis, held in October 1955.[1] Not that Warburg had stopped publishing new variations of his experimental set-up, which always gave the same high quantum yields. In reaction to Warburg's then most recent papers, Gaffron wrote the following letter to Burk in March 1956:

Dear Dean

I delayed this note of thanks until we had sent you our recent papers in reciprocation of your kindness in forwarding us the latest reprints from Warburg's laboratory. These publications on photosynthesis have now clarified the situation rather definitely: "Too strong tobacco to smoke in my Meershaum!" [sic] The deviations from the experiments and theories of other workers in the field are wonderfully clear. Soon there will be no need to concern oneself with the matter any further.

What I am wondering is to what extent you personally are willing to believe in and subscribe to what comes from Dahlem? For us it would simplify the situation if we were allowed to identify you entirely with the Warburg school, but I cannot help feeling that this might do you a serious injustice. You should feel young enough to dare to deviate from the party doctrine the moment you recognize how absurd the tenets are in which followers are asked to believe. Has that moment arrived?

---

[1] The papers of this conference were published in the volume Gaffron, Brown, Stacy, Livingston, Rabinowitch, Strehler & Tolbert (1957).

Very sincerely yours, Hans G. Gaffron.[2]

Gaffron's disbelief and consternation concerned, among other things, Warburg's claim (first published at the end of 1954) that, in order to compensate for respiration, no high intensity white background light was necessary, as he had believed up to then, but that blue or green light beams of rather small intensity were sufficient, the effect of which Warburg called "catalytic".[3] Despite the fact that many of the players were tired of the maximum quantum yield question, this paper was nevertheless broadly discussed. Thus, the Stanford-based plant physiologist Lawrence Blinks (1900–1989) wrote to Emerson on 28 September, 1955: *"What do you think of Warburg and Krippahl's strange findings on blue light (after red)? I've never tried exactly that experiment, but I now aim to, on Ulva or Monostroma. Off hand, I don't believe it, but strange things do happen."*[4] Emerson replied to him on 10 October, 1955:

> *As for Warburg's blue light experiments, the wave length is about the same as that in which Tony Lewis and I found evidence of strong effects of light on respiration. I've tried to think of an interpretation that would account for both our observations and Warburg's, but they don't seem to agree. Warburg's manometry has become almost mystical, and I'm generally pretty skeptical of his interpretations, but I do believe there are some special effects of certain wave lengths of blue light. I'll be interested to hear what you find with Ulva and Monostroma. We hope to do some experiments with Chlorella and Porphyridium, as soon as we are satisfied with our measurements of light absorption.*[5]

The experiments on the effect of combining lights of different colors foreshadowed a fruitful line of research that Emerson pursued in the second half of the 1950s. In December 1955, Emerson wrote to Hill to inform him that he was now working again on photosynthesis efficiencies at different wavelengths of light, *"a subject that warms my enthusiasm quite a bit more than the problems of two-vessel manometry. Maybe we shall come to trying some mixtures of blue and red light, though when one looks closely at Warburg's data, it seems that there is no clear evidence*

---

[2]Archive of the BBAW, NL Warburg 174. Gaffron to Burk, 7 March 1956. The correct spelling of the German word would be "Meerschaum", which is

[3]Warburg, Krippahl & Schröder (1954). See also Warburg, Krippahl & Schröder (1955) for an extension of this new idea.

[4]Blinks to Emerson, 28 Sept. 1955, Robert Emerson Papers, 1923-61, Record Series 15/4/28, Box 1, Folder: Blinks, Haxo, University of Illinois Archives. *Ulva* and *Monostroma* are genera of (multicellular) green algae.

[5]Emerson to Blinks, 10 Oct. 1955, Robert Emerson Papers, 1923-61, Record Series 15/4/28, Box 1, Folder: Blinks, Haxo, University of Illinois Archives.

Figure V.1: Eugene Rabinowitch in the late 1950s. (Photograph provided by Govindjee.)

for the special effect of blue."[6] One can take from his correspondence that Emerson did indeed take up this line of research, which led him to make an unexpected discovery. A first indication of this discovery can be taken from a letter that Emerson wrote to William Arnold on 9 April, 1956: *"The significance of the long-wave limit is becoming very interesting. Accessory illumination with shorter wave lengths makes the increment of photosynthesis attainable with very long wave lengths higher than it is without accessory illumination".*[7] A week later, on 16 April 1956, Emerson wrote to Franck, informing him of the same as well as adding the following assertion:

> *The amounts of accessory light required are considerable – larger than the amounts of the red beams being used. "Catalytic" amounts of accessory light are not sufficient. The accessory light may be red, green, or blue. We do not yet know what would be the effect of large intensities of the region 670-700 mμ [nm], because we have no suitable filters for isolating an accessory beam of this range. We have ordered some filters, but I am not sure they will give us enough energy. It is difficult to isolate this region without contamination of shorter wave lengths.*

---

[6]Cambridge University Library, Ms. Add. 9267/J.54. Emerson to Hill, Dec. 26, 1955.

[7]Emerson to Arnold, 9 April 1956, Robert Emerson Papers, 1923-61, Record Series 15/4/28, Box 1, Folder: Arnold, William, University of Illinois Archives.

This letter should reach you by Wednesday. I plan to telephone you
Thursday morning at about 10 o'clock. Please excuse the brevity
of this rather hasty letter. I should be setting up an experiment.[8]

Emerson was clearly excited about his findings and urgently requested
Franck's opinion and advice; at the same time, he was anxious, already
then, to differentiate between his findings and Warburg's catalytic effect
of blue and green light. Emerson presented a preliminary account of his
work at the annual meeting of the US National Academy of Science,
between 23 to 25 April 1956.[9] Therein, he noted, first, that at higher
temperatures photosynthetic efficiency dropped at shorter wavelengths.
This was a blow to the assumption that the drop in photosynthetic
efficiency at low-intensity light of the far red was due to the fact that
the light quanta of this region had insufficient energy. In this case, the
increase in temperature should have improved the quantum yield – yet
the opposite was the case. The second surprising discovery reported by
Emerson and co-workers was the following: *"If the low-intensity light*
beam of measured energy is supplemented by a more intense (unmeasured)
beam, then the efficiency of the small increment of measured light remains
nearly constant out to 685 mμ [nm], even at a temperature of 26° C".

By November, 1956, Emerson had put the results of the year's work
into manuscript form, which he mailed off to the Proceedings of the
National Academy of Sciences (PNAS). It was circulated in advance to
Gaffron, Arnold, Briggs and Hill, which left Emerson without any more
spare copies, although he would also have liked to send one to Blinks for
comments. (Blinks had, together with Francis Haxo (1921–2010), also
found a long wavelength decline in the photosynthesis efficiency of green
and brown algae, which they suggested might be because sections of
the chlorophyll might be inactive.[10]) In his letter to Blinks, Emerson
described the content of his paper as follows:

I have proposed an interpretation which I think fits your results
on red, brown, and green algae, as well as some new observa-
tions of ours. I believe my interpretation is the nearest thing to
an "idea" that I have ever produced in my life. It is speculative,
and Rabinowitch was at first inclined to be very doubtful of its
value. Recently he said he thought it the most plausible alternative
he could think of for explaining observations up to the present

---

[8]Emerson to Franck, 16 April 1956, Robert Emerson Papers, 1923-61, Record Series
15/4/28, Box 1, Folder: Franck, James, University of Illinois Archives.

[9]See the abstract of the paper, published as Emerson, Chalmers, Cederstrand &
Brody (1956).

[10]Cf. Haxo & Blinks (1950); for a tribute to Lawrence R. Blinks, see Thorhaug &
Berlyn (2009).

time, but he hopes that new evidence will suggest other and more acceptable interpretations.

I am suggesting that photosynthesis requires excitation of some pigment in addition to chlorophyll a, *with an energy level higher than the first excited state of chlorophyll* a. *This would account for the low yield when chlorophyll* a *is the sole light absorber, as far as green algae are concerned. Chlorophyll* b *would be the pigment with a higher excitation level. In brown algae it might be chlorophyll* c *or fucoxanthol. In reds and blue-greens it would be a phycobilin, or combination of phycobilins. It seems to me this promises to account for the observed limits of full photosynthetic efficiency in all cases. Rabinowitch is concerned because it fails to account for the decline in yield of fluorescence on the long-wave side of the chlorophyll* a *absorption band, a phenomenon which he feels should have a common basis with the decline in yield of photosynthesis in the same spectral region.*[11]

Rabinowitch was, indeed, concerned and skeptical about the proposed interpretation; yet Emerson's paper on *Chlorella* was published in the PNAS as Emerson, Chalmers & Cederstrand (1957). It had been known since the work done by Emerson and Lewis in 1943 that at low light intensities, photosynthetic efficiency dropped at wavelengths above 685 nm, although chlorophyll *a* absorption was still appreciable; now Emerson had found, with Ruth Chalmers and Carl Cederstrand, that the yield under these conditions could be improved by supplementary light of shorter wavelengths. The limit of wavelengths that were still effective as a supplement was identified to be somewhere between 644 and 680 nm. Considerable emphasis, again, was put on the fact that this phenomenon was very different from the catalytic blue light effect reported by Warburg et al. (1954).[12]

The tentative explanation given in the paper was the one Emerson had outlined in his letter to Blinks. Emerson, Chalmers and Cederstrand (1957) suggested that *"the significance of the supplementary light may be that it adds excitation of other pigments besides chlorophyll* a. *The maintenance of maximum efficiency may require the excitation of some*

---

[11]Emerson to Blinks, 30 Nov. 1956, Robert Emerson Papers, 1923-61, Record Series 15/4/28, Box 1, Folder: Blinks, Haxo, University of Illinois Archives.

[12]This discussion of Warburg's work was critically remarked upon, in advance to publication, by Gaffron, to which Emerson replied: *"As for Warburg, I agree with you that our reference to his work with supplementary light will lead to controversy, but I do not feel it would be right for us to report work with supplementary light, without at least a reference to his work. This is the sort of thing he does to us all the time, and the least I can do is set him a good example."* Emerson to Gaffron, 14 Dec. 1956, Robert Emerson Papers, 1923-61, Record Series 15/4/28, Box 1, Folder: Gaffron, Hans, University of Illinois Archives.

pigment with an absorption band corresponding to an energy level higher than the first excited state of chlorophyll a."[13] In the green algae this pigment might be chlorophyll *b*. The authors openly acknowledged the fact that this interpretation did not conform to other recent notions concerning the energy transfer in photosynthesis:

> *[This interpretation] is in conflict with the widely accepted view that transfer of excitation energy to chlorophyll* a *from other pigments takes place with practically 100 per cent efficiency [cited Duysens (1952)]. It also fails to account for the reduced yield of fluorescence on the long-wave side of the absorption band of chlorophyll* a. *However, if further work should confirm our suggestion that photosynthesis requires excitation of two different pigments, we can hardly expect to find a common interpretation for the long-wave decline in yield of fluorescence and photosynthesis.*

Emerson undoubtedly realized that these were not minor points; he would have preferred to come up with an interpretation that gave a common cause for both phenomena: the drop in photosynthesis efficiency and the drop in chlorophyll *a* fluorescence. However, he was unable to find one, as he wrote in a letter to Franck on 22 January 1957.[14] Emerson and his co-workers continued their investigation of the enhancement effect. In the first months of 1957, they focused mainly on the influence of intensity and wavelength on the supplementary light; besides his general wish to explore the effect and its causal context in more detail, Emerson was probably still driven by the goal to distinguish his supplementary light effect from Warburg's idea of catalytic blue light effects – which, in the meantime, he had also advertised in Warburg (1958). This difference between Warburg's work and his own was also emphasized in Emerson's subsequent presentations, in 1957 and 1958, at the meetings of the US National Academy of Science.[15] Under no circumstances did Emerson want to be cited as confirming Warburg's results, although he did acknowledge that he had hit upon the phenomenon in question while double-checking the catalytic light claim. In July 1957, Emerson wrote to Hill: *"I've had quite an exciting time with the experiments on mixing long-wave light with shorter wave lengths. The effects do not match Warburg's claims at*

---

[13]This and the following quote: Emerson et al. (1957), p. 142.

[14]Emerson to Franck, 22 Jan. 1957. Robert Emerson Papers, 1923-61, Record Series 15/4/28, Box 1, Folder: Franck, James, University of Illinois Archives.

[15]See the abstract of the 1957 talk in *Science* as Emerson (1957); Robert Emerson was the sole author, although his collaborative work with Chalmers and Cederstrand was acknowledged. The failure to replicate Warburg's findings was repeated again in Emerson's presentation at the 1958 NAS meeting; see the abstract Emerson (1958*b*).

Figure V.2: A gathering of the Urbana group in 1958. Left to right: Thomas (Tom) T. Bannister (a student of Rabinowitch, who had passed his doctoral exam), Mary Jeanne Bannister (wife of Tom), Ruth V. Chalmers (assistant of Emerson, holding a Champaign bottle), Tita Emerson (wife of Robert Emerson), Eugene Rabinowitch, Rajni Govindjee (student of Emerson), Robert Emerson, Marcia Brody (student of Emerson) and Steve Brody (student of Rabinowitch). (Photograph was taken by Govindjee.)

all, but of course we were stimulated to do the experiments because of Warburg's claims."[16]

In 1958, Emerson gave a talk at the annual meeting of the Phycological Society of America, where he showed the action spectra of the Enhancement Effect in *Chlorella* (i.e. a green alga), *Navicula* (a diatom), *Anacystis* (a cyanobacterium) and *Porphyridium* (a red alga), when one of the two light beams was kept constant in the far-red region, and the wavelength of the second beam was varied.[17] A summary of this lecture was published as Emerson & Chalmers (1958) without the figures. The main conclusion was that photosynthesis is run by two pigment systems, one being chlorophyll *a*, and the other an auxiliary pigment, which is chlorophyll *b* in *Chlorella*; fucoxanthin and chlorophyll *c* in *Navicula*; phycoerythrin and phycocyanin in *Porphyridium*; and phycocyanin in *Anacystis*. (Similar results were included in Emerson (1958a), which presented a review of the field.) However, this conclusion had to be modified later, particularly by the work of one of us (Govindjee).[18]

---

[16]Cambridge University Library, Ms. Add. 9267/J.54. Emerson to Hill, 6 July 1957.

[17]This is remembered by one of us (G), who had attended this lecture.

[18]The error became obvious from the work done by Govindjee, Rajni Govindjee and Eugene Rabinowitch (see below); an overview of the research done along these lines is also given in Govindjee & Björn (2011).

2   Emerson's Death and Beyond

On 4 February 1959, Emerson died in an aeroplane crash. According to his friend and colleague Rabinowitch, Emerson had always distrusted aviation as a means of transport and preferred to travel around the country by train. It was only because the train service from Indianapolis to New York had been discontinued in the late 1950s that he had grudgingly turned to flying between Chicago and New York. This particular time, Emerson was on his way to attend a meeting at Harvard University. Even more tragic was the fact that Emerson was originally booked on another flight; yet when he arrived at Chicago, a flight that had been delayed was still waiting to depart for New York. At the last minute Emerson transferred to it, hoping that he would arrive at his destination a little earlier.[19] This turned out to be a fatal decision.

Emerson left behind a great deal of experimental material at the Urbana laboratory, accumulated during the years that he had been working on the long-wave limit of photosynthesis; only some of this work was published posthumously, in 1960, by Emerson's friend and Urbana colleague Rabinowitch.[20] It was in this publication that the phenomenon in question – the effect that supplementary light of shorter wavelengths is able to make up for the drop in photosynthetic efficiency at longer wavelengths – was called, for the first time, the *"(second) Emerson effect"* (while the carbon dioxide burst was named the *"first Emerson effect"*). In this 1960 paper, Rabinowitch duly presented Emerson's data, although he argued against the assumption that the phenomenon was due to a direct contribution of chlorophyll *b* in photosynthesis: Rabinowitch believed that the evidence derived from fluorescence experiments, which demonstrated that a large fraction of the quanta absorbed by chlorophyll *b* was transferred to chlorophyll *a* by resonance, made this highly unlikely. He suggested, as an alternative, that two types of chlorophyll *a* were present in the living cell, one of which accepted more excitation energy from chlorophyll *b* than the other, while the other was unable to sensitize photosynthesis to its maximum quantum yield.

The question was pursued further by Emerson's two remaining doctoral students, Govindjee and Rajni Govindjee, both of whom were involved in projects related to the supplementary light – or enhancement – effect. Together with Rabinowitch, Govindjee succeeded in establishing the existence of two forms of chlorophyll *a*, which had distinct functions in the photosynthetic process in algal cells.[21] They showed that a short

---

[19]Cf. Rabinowitch (1961), p. 126.

[20]See Emerson & Rabinowitch (1960).

[21]This was published by Govindjee & Rabinowitch (1960) and Rabinowitch & Govindjee (1961).

wavelength absorbing form of chlorophyll a was in the same system as chlorophyll b, whereas a long wavelength absorbing form of chlorophyll a was assumed to be in the other system. C. Stacy French came to a similar conclusion.[22] Together with the biophysicist Jan B. Thomas and Rabinowitch, Rajni Govindjee was able to establish, in *Chlorella* cells, whose respiration was inhibited by a para-benzoquinone system, that the enhancement effect was a real phenomenon in photosynthesis: it was not an artifact; it was not caused by respiration; and it was not associated with the carbon dioxide reduction process.[23] All the new results gave figures of 8 to 10 quanta as a minimum requirement for the release of one oxygen molecule. This number was reconfirmed in R. Govindjee, Rabinowitch & Govindjee (1968), when the authors made an ultimate attempt to replicate those conditions and materials that Warburg had specified in his (then) latest papers, that is, the use of blue catalytic light, 10 % carbon dioxide and young synchronous *Chlorella* cultures. In the same year, Ng & Bassham (1968) published a minimum value of 9 to 12 quanta per oxygen in *Chlorella* cells, by measuring both oxygen release and carbon dioxide uptake: this clearly confirmed Emerson's results, not Warburg's (although neither Emerson nor anybody else from the Urbana group was mentioned in this paper). Similar findings were obtained in experiments carried out long after that period. *Chlorella* cells were re-examined by Ley & Mauzerall (1982), while Skillman (2008) presented the results of quantum yield experiments in various types of plants, using three different pathways of carbon dioxide fixation. None of these experiments has ever yielded anything less than a requirement of 8 quanta per molecule of oxygen, so that the controversy can safely be considered settled: not only theoretically, but experimentally.

However, in the meantime the field had moved on. The curious enhancement phenomenon and the emergence of different forms and functions of chlorophyll triggered a wealth of related investigations. More and more findings were accumulated, the interpretation of which again became the subject of intense debate; while the question of determining the maximum quantum yield of photosynthesis gradually faded from the scene. While Warburg seemed to believe that Emerson's death had decided the matter in his favor – he was overheard stating this in public[24] – the real reason was that the question had lost its attraction and importance.

---

[22] See French (1961).

[23] See R. Govindjee, Thomas & Rabinowitch (1960).

[24] Govindjee (personal communication) was recounted this episode by Rabinowitch, on his return from a conference held at Gif-sur-Yvette (south-west of Paris) in 1963.

3   EPILOGUE: LONG AFTER EMERSON'S DEATH

In 1969, Warburg was invited to contribute a paper to the American Journal of Botany, which then was published as Warburg, Krippahl & Lehman (1969). In its abstract, the authors wrote:

> *For calculation of the true quantum requirement of photosynthesis from experimental measurements, it is necessary to measure the light absorbed by the photolyte only, since the light energy absorbed by free chlorophyll is not used in the oxygen development of photosynthesis. To eliminate the loss of the light absorbed by the free chlorophyll, the factor e = photolyte/total chlorophyll must be introduced into the calculation. Failure to take e into consideration has led to discrepancies of 1,000 % between the quantum yields obtained in different laboratories. These discrepancies are now removed. The quantum requirement of the splitting of the photolyte is always 1.*[25]

According to this paper, Warburg et al. (1969) had measured, by the usual method, i.e., determining the number of quanta absorbed per oxygen molecule evolved, a value of approximately 12 quanta per oxygen at the lowest light intensity used. It is noteworthy that this now, after thirty years of divergence, was in perfect agreement with measurements taken by Warburg's alleged enemies. However, Warburg et al. (1969) thought otherwise. They declared that the *Chlorella* cells contained a large amount of "free" chlorophyll, which was photochemically inert; thus, the quantum requirement had to be obtained not from the total amount of chlorophyll but only from the amount of "photolyte" contained in the cell, which the authors conceived of as a complex of chlorophyll bound to carbonic acid. The concept of this "photolyte", as the reacting unit in photosynthesis, goes right back to Warburg's first papers on photosynthesis, such as Warburg (1919), Warburg (1920) and Warburg (1921); however, this complex was never substantiated to exist. Furthermore, in 1969, it had long been accepted that in photosynthesis carbon dioxide was neither photochemically split, nor directly reduced to the stage of carbohydrates; but rather fed into a complex reaction cycle that had been discovered by a research team in Berkeley, headed by Melvin Calvin and Andrew A. Benson.[26] None of this seems to have been accepted by Warburg, who still clung to his photolyte idea.

The number of photolyte complexes had to be obtained in a very complicated manner based on oxygen measurements. Using this method,

---

[25]Warburg et al. (1969), p. 961.

[26]See, e.g., Bassham, Benson, Kay, Harris, Wilson & Calvin (1954) for one of the decisive papers; also see Benson (2002a) for details on the discovery.

Warburg et al. (1969) calculated the minimum quantum requirement of photosynthesis at all light intensities to be 3 – which was quite remarkable, indeed. However, it was in fine agreement with Warburg's earlier publications that had calculated the quantum requirement without differentiating between free chlorophyll and photolyte. It was definitely not in agreement with measurements taken elsewhere – while from the paper itself it was totally unclear to which measurements, laboratories or publications the authors referred, when they mentioned in the abstract "discrepancies of 1,000 % between the quantum yields obtained in different laboratories", since the only references given in Warburg et al. (1969) were six papers co-authored by Warburg himself. Not one publication by Emerson or anybody else is referred to, not even as the target of specific criticism.

Govindjee (1999) has evaluated this 1969 paper, and has placed it in perspective of the field at that time. It seems that Warburg was still convinced that Einstein's Law of Photochemical Equivalence was the key to understanding photosynthesis; and since water oxidation required removal of 4 electrons to release one molecule of oxygen, the minimum quantum requirement in photosynthesis had to be 4 light quanta per oxygen. It is very probable that, had Warburg accepted – as most people had since around 1960 – that there were two light reactions and two pigment systems in photosynthesis, he also would have accepted a minimum quantum requirement of 8 per oxygen. Instead, Warburg et al. (1969) stated: *"We do not hesitate to express here our satisfaction that after the short time of 46 years [cited Warburg & Negelein (1923)] truth has now won its war also in the main reaction of bioenergetics"* (p. 967). Even if there ever had been a "war" to be won, it surely would have ceased to exist after this paper of 1969 – yet, the "victory" was not Warburg's. As Govindjee (1999) put it:

> *The authors [i.e. Warburg, Krippahl and Lehman] failed to emphasize that their new measurements were in agreement with the measurements of Emerson. No one had doubted the validity of Einstein's law: the two light reaction scheme is in agreement with the measured quantum requirement values of 8 at low light intensities not only of Emerson and coworkers (including Arnold 1949; and R. Govindjee et al. 1968), but, we emphasize, Warburg himself.*[27]

---

[27]Govindjee (1999), p. 253.

Chapter VI

CONCLUDING REMARKS

While in the second half of the 1950s Warburg's work on quantum yields was increasingly criticized elsewhere, in his own country he was still regarded as the leading authority in the field of photosynthesis research. Presumably, this was at least partly due to the fact that Warburg published predominantly in German journals, which, at the time, in Germany were far more widely read (since they were more easily available) than their American or British counterparts. The resulting picture was inevitably skewed. Another factor may have been of a psychological nature: In the spirit of self-pity prevailing in the postwar years, many Germans (particularly non-experts) were inclined to frame the controversy between Warburg and the photosynthesis researchers in the United States and Great Britain in political terms, as another aspect of the unjustified repression of Germans by the allied "invaders".[1]

However, Warburg received a strong blow to his authority when in 1961 it was not Warburg who received the Nobel Prize for Chemistry, honoring his work in photosynthesis, but rather the chemist Melvin Calvin, that is, one of Warburg's stubborn opponents.[2] In the announcement of the year's Nobel Prizes, in December 1961, the German weekly magazine Spiegel gave a sarcastic report of the situation. It was described, how in 1957, Warburg had proudly declared in a public lecture that, thanks to his work, Germany had been able to maintain its international leadership in photosynthesis research, despite the Second World War and the country's collapse.[3] The decision of the Nobel Prize Committee to award the Chemistry Prize to Calvin and not Warburg only four years later was felt to be in stark – and disillusioning – contrast to the pompous self-confidence of Warburg's. Now, slowly, Germany began to realize that Warburg, through ignoring the work done in other laboratories, had become more and more isolated within the international scientific community and that, as a consequence, his contributions were increasingly off the mark.

---

[1]On the atmosphere among scientists in postwar Germany, see, e.g., Deichmann (2001a) (which focuses on biochemists) or Hentschel (2005) (on physicists).

[2]Note, however, that in our opinion, Andrew A. Benson (*1916) had made key contributions to the work for which Calvin had received the Nobel Prize; see, e.g., Govindjee (2010) for a tribute to Benson. Benson's 90th birthday was celebrated through a special issue of the journal Photosynthesis Research (see Buchanan, Douce & Lichtenthaler (2007)) and a dinner on October 24, 2007, at the Le Procope restaurant in Paris, France; see Lichtenthaler, Buchanan & Douce (2008).

[3]Cf. Anonymous (1961).

Although Warburg seemed undisturbed by these developments, and would still claim in his publications of 1970 (the year of his death) that he had solved the problem of photosynthesis, the late biochemist Birgit Vennesland (1913–2001) recorded and passed on to the public the following remarkable quotation. When Vennesland asked Warburg whether he had made any mistakes in his life, he replied:

> *Of course, I have made mistakes – many of them. The only way to avoid making any mistakes is never to do anything at all. My biggest mistake was to get much too much involved in controversy. Never get involved in controversy. It's a waste of time. It isn't that controversy itself is wrong. No, it can be even stimulating. But controversy takes too much time and energy. That's what's wrong about it. I have wasted my time and energy in controversy, when I should have been going on doing new experiments.*[4]

Since Emerson also felt that he had spent too much time and energy on the quantum yield controversy,[5] and so did almost everyone else working around them, one should think that the controversy could have ended much earlier. However, if one recalls, first, the importance of the question, and, second, the enormous complexity of the experiments, it seems doubtful that the issue could have been settled without an extended debate after the first attempts in the late 1930s, even if Warburg would have stayed out of it – although, of course, the discussion would have been much more amicable without Warburg's biting remarks; and Emerson as well as many others could have saved a lot of time for more fruitful experimentation since they would not have had to try and reproduce Warburg's ever changing set-ups. However, as late as 1960, Bessel Kok stated, in a comprehensive paper on the problem of the maximum quantum yield of photosynthesis: *"Preponderate evidence seems to support the generalisation that at least eight quanta are required per one O_2 evolved"*; to which, however, he regretfully added: *"It is rather dissatisfying that 25 years after Warburg and Negelein's first estimations we cannot justify more firmly stated conclusions."*[6]

However, notwithstanding these remaining uncertainties, hardly anybody was interested in continuing the debate. As was mentioned earlier, already Brown & Frenkel (1953) had strongly pleaded that the controversy be resolved using other methods. Attention has also been drawn to the fact that the second Gatlinburg Conference on Photosynthesis of 1955, which was explicitly devoted to the discussion of the

---

[4]Quoted in Govindjee (2004), p. 185; see Vennesland (1981).
[5]Cf. Walker (1997), p. 8.
[6]Kok (1960), p. 623.

most pressing issues in photosynthesis research, deliberately excluded any discussion of the maximum quantum yield. It was also in 1955 that Warburg requested, once again, that the question be settled by an officially implemented, *"impartial"* committee. It is difficult to interpret Warburg's motivation behind this idea. The easiest, albeit non-charitable, answer is that one person (or a small group of people) can be more conveniently worked on than the large and uncontrollable scientific community as such. The chances of success for a person such as Warburg, willing to apply appropriate techniques of persuasion, was comparatively high – and even if the impartial observers were not fully convinced, it would be simple for Warburg to take advantage of any uncertainties. However, more charitable alternatives are conceivable, although it is hard to imagine that Warburg was naïve enough to think that a sustainable solution could have been advanced by this Prussian way of arriving at a top-down truth sentence on a scientific question. The response of the scientific community, which was represented by the members of the National Academy of Science of the United States to which Warburg's request for an impartial committee was forwarded, was unambiguous. Warburg's appeal that an authoritative committee take charge was on no account acceptable – scientific controversies had to be resolved by the scientific community, in a democratic manner, so to speak. And this is exactly what happened: Franck dealt with the question from the point of view of theoretical physics and photochemistry, Emerson tried to sort out the problems that arose from the technique of manometry, while Arnold and others developed alternative methods to revisit the question independently. The huge amount of correspondence that was generated and the highly increased frequency of meetings aptly reflects the participants' wish to solve the problem in a cooperative manner.

What made this so difficult was the fact that those people who were directly involved in the debate had started to distrust both Warburg and Burk. At the beginning of 1955, Gaffron wrote to Franck that he had received a letter from Emerson stating that although Emerson had again faithfully reproduced the latest experimental set-up specified by Warburg, he had obtained no change in resulting quantum yields. Gaffron commented:

> He [Emerson] can't understand Warburg's results – and neither can I, of course. Unless one leaves the realm of science and says: since he [Warburg] lies anyway – he lies consciously when citing other people – why not also here? If his set-up has been worked on for so long, that it yields inaccurate results automatically, who will be able to detect this, without taking everything apart and building it up again, piece by piece. [Carl] Neuberg, who always lied, and

*may therefore be considered an expert in this matter, said, if one
fails to prove that he [Warburg] has been deceiving us, then he will
have won.*[7]

Emerson had likewise come to believe that not everybody was playing
by the rules. When Warburg claimed, in 1954, to have found low quantum
yields in a carbonate buffer solution, Emerson was persuaded that there
was a flaw in his methods, although it had been carefully concealed; and
he suspected the same of any other surprising data that originated from
Warburg's laboratory. On 20 May, 1954, Emerson wrote to Daniels:

*I feel as you do that maybe someone ought to check on Warburg's
electrometric results, but I think there is a limit to what we can
accomplish by checking each fantastic claim as it comes along. I'm
afraid I have built up a prejudice against Warburg's experimental
work, because of his abuse of the manometric technique, and I
tend to feel that if I took the time I would find a joker in his
electrometric measurements as well. One cannot print this sort
of thing, of course, nor say it for the record. However, for the
present I think I shall let the electrometric results alone, and see
what I can find through further study of the transients as revealed
by manometric measurements.*[8]

These sentiments were shared by a number of other people, and
Warburg's reputation suffered accordingly. For example, his finding that
very small amounts of carbon dioxide were necessary for photosynthesis
to function was unjustifiably swept aside.[9] It was only when Warburg
raised the issue of the curious effects of blue light that Emerson became
truly interested in the former's work again, but this was because the
publication reminded Emerson how, many years earlier, Lewis and he had
also found that the light in this region had strange effects, for example
on the course of respiration, although they had never cared to scrutinize

---

[7]Gaffron to Franck, dated 2 Feb. Franck, James. Papers, [Box 3, Folder 7], Special
Collections Research Center, University of Chicago Library. The year 1955 was
reconstructed from the description of Warburg's setup, namely catalytic use of blue
or green light, which Warburg had first announced in Warburg et al. (1954).

[8]Emerson to Daniels, 20 May 1954, Robert Emerson Papers, 1923-61, Record Series
15/4/28, Box 1, Folder: Daniels, Farrington, University of Illinois Archives.

[9]However, this effect has been established to be between the two photosystems, and
not on the mechanism of oxygen evolution, as Warburg had suggested. See Stemler
(2002) for a short review of the so-called bicarbonate effect, discovered originally in
Warburg & Krippahl (1958), and the detrimental effect Warburg's reputation had on
the reception of this phenomenon. The bicarbonate effect became an important theme
of research; it was predominantly pursued in Govindjee's laboratory at Urbana, and
was the theme of seven PhD theses that he supervised. See, e.g., Van Rensen, Xu &
Govindjee (1999) for a survey of this work.

it in detail. Warburg's finding thus prompted Emerson to return to this phenomenon, for which he used Warburg's two-light beam approach. And luckily so, one might add, for otherwise Emerson would not have hit upon the Enhancement Effect.

We close this little book by citing a penetrative limerick, written by an anonymous contemporary of Warburg's, which requires no additional comment:

There was a great scientist named Otto

who lived by the following motto:

"I am always right!

My enemies I'll fight.

(But I'll be glad to send them my photo.)"[10]

---

[10]Quoted in Höxtermann & Sucker (1989), p. 106.

References

ANONYMOUS (1961), 'Grünes Geheimnis', *Der Spiegel* **48**, 88–89.

ARNOLD, W. (1935), *Investigations on photosynthesis*. PhD Thesis, Harvard University, Cambridge (Massachusetts).

ARNOLD, W. (1949), A Calorimetric Determination of the Quantum Yield in Photosynthesis, *in* J. FRANCK & W. E. LOOMIS, Ed., 'Photosynthesis in Plants', Iowa State College Press, Ames, Iowa, pp. 273–276.

ARNOLD, W. (1991), 'Experiments', *Photosynthesis Research* **27**, 73–82.

BAGGOT, J. (2010), *The First War of Physics: The Secret History of the Atom Bomb, 1939–1949*, Pegasus.

BANNISTER, T. T. (1972), 'The careers and contributions of Eugene Rabinow-itch', *Biophysical Journal* **12**, 707–718.

BASSHAM, J. A., BENSON, A. A., KAY, L. D., HARRIS, A. Z., WILSON, A. T. & CALVIN, M. (1954), 'The path of carbon in photosynthesis. XXI. The cyclic regeneration of carbon dioxide acceptor', *Journal of the American Chemical Society* **76**, 1760–1770.

BENSON, A. A. (2002*a*), 'Following the path of carbon in photosynthesis: a personal story', *Photosynthesis Research* **73**, 29–49.

BENSON, A. A. (2002*b*), 'Paving the path', *Annual Review of Plant Biology* **53**, 1–25.

BEYERCHEN, A. D. (1996), Emigration from Country and Discipline: The Journey of a German Physicist into American Photosynthesis Research, *in* M. G. ASH & A. SÖLLNER, Ed., 'Forced Migration and Scientific Change', Cambridge University Press, Cambridge, Mass., pp. 71–85.

BLACKMAN, F. F. (1905), 'Optima and limiting factors', *Annals of Botany* **19**, 281–295.

BLANKENSHIP, R. E. (2002), *Molecular Mechanisms of Photosynthesis*, Blackwell.

BROWN, A. H. (1953), 'The effects of light on respiration, using isotopically enriched oxygen', *American Journal of Botany* **40**, 719–729.

BROWN, A. H. & FRENKEL, A. W. (1953), 'Photosynthesis', *Annual Review of Biochemistry* **22**, 423–458.

BROWN, A. H. & GOOD, N. (1955), 'Photochemical reduction of oxygen in chloroplast preparations and in green plant cells. I. The study of oxygen exchanges *in vitro* and *in vivo*', *Archives of Biochemistry and Biophysics* **57**, 340–354.

BROWN, A. H. & WHITTINGHAM, C. P. (1955), 'Identification of the carbon dioxide burst in Chlorella using the recording mass spectrometer', *Plant Physiology* **30**, 231–237.

BROWN, H. T. & ESCOMBE, F. (1905), 'Researches on some of the physiological processes of green leaves, with special reference to the interchange of energy between the leaf and its surroundings', *Proceedings of the Royal Society of London, Series B* **76**(507), 29–111.

BUCHANAN, B. B., DOUCE, R. & LICHTENTHALER, H. K., Eds. (2007), *A Tribute to Andrew A. Benson*. Special issue of Photosynthesis Research (Vol. 92, pp. 143-271).

BURK, D., CORNFIELD, J. & SCHWARTZ, M. (1951), 'The efficient transformation of light into chemical energy in photosynthesis', *The Scientific Monthly* **73**, 213–223.

BURK, D., HENDRICKS, S., KORZENOVSKY, M., SCHOCKEN, V. & WARBURG, O. (1949), 'The maximum efficiency of photosynthesis: A rediscovery', *Science* **110**, 225–229.

CLAYTON, R. K. (1965), *Molecular Physics in Photosynthesis*, Blaisdell, New York.

DEICHMANN, U. (2001*a*), The Expulsion of German-Jewish Chemists and Biochemists and their Correspondence with Colleagues in Germany after 1945: The Impossibility of Normalization?, *in* M. SZÖLLÖSI-JANZE, Ed., 'Science in the Third Reich', Berg, Oxford/New York, pp. 243–280.

DEICHMANN, U. (2001*b*), *Flüchten, Mitmachen, Vergessen. Chemiker und Biochemiker in der NS Zeit*, Wiley VCH.

DUYSENS, L. N. M. (1952), Transfer of excitation energy in photosynthesis, Ph.d., University of Utrecht, Netherlands.

DUYSENS, L. N. M. (1989), 'The discovery of the two photosynthetic systems: a personal account', *Photosynthesis Research* **21**, 61–79.

EINSTEIN, A. (1912*a*), 'Nachtrag zu meiner Arbeit: "Thermodynamische Begründung des photochemischen Aequivalentgesetzes"', *Annalen der Physik* **38**, 881–884.

EINSTEIN, A. (1912*b*), 'Thermodynamische Begründung des photochemischen Aequivalentgesetzes', *Annalen der Physik* **37**, 832–838.

EMERSON, R. (1957), 'Dependence of the yield of photosynthesis in long-wave red on wavelength and intensity of supplementary light', *Science* **125**, 746.

EMERSON, R. (1958*a*), 'The quantum yield of photosynthesis', *Annual Review of Plant Physiology* **9**, 1–24.

EMERSON, R. (1958*b*), 'Yield of photosynthesis from simultaneous illumination with pairs of wavelengths. Abstract, paper presented at the 1958 annual meeting of the National Academy of Sciences', *Science* **127**, 1059–1060.

EMERSON, R. & ARNOLD, W. (1932), 'The photochemical reaction in photosynthesis', *Journal of General Physiology* **16**, 191–205.

EMERSON, R. & CHALMERS, R. (1955), 'Transient changes in cellular gas exchange and the problem of maximum efficiency of photosynthesis', *Plant Physiology* **30**, 504–529.

EMERSON, R. & CHALMERS, R. (1958), 'Speculations concerning the function and phylogenetic significance of the accessory pigments of algae', *Phycological Society of America News Bulletin* **11**, 51–56.

EMERSON, R. & LEWIS, C. M. (1939), 'Factors influencing the efficiency of photosynthesis', *American Journal of Botany* **26**(10), 808–822.

EMERSON, R. & LEWIS, C. M. (1941), 'Carbon dioxide exchange and the measurement of the quantum yield of photosynthesis', *American Journal of Botany* **28**, 789–804.

EMERSON, R. & LEWIS, C. M. (1943), 'The dependence of the quantum yield of Chlorella photosynthesis on wave length of light', *American Journal of Botany* **30**, 165–178.

EMERSON, R. & RABINOWITCH, E. I. (1960), 'Red drop and role of auxiliary pigments in photosynthesis', *Plant Physiology* **35**, 477–485.

EMERSON, R., CHALMERS, R., CEDERSTRAND, C. & BRODY, M. (1956), 'Effect of temperature on the long-wave limit of photosynthesis', *Science* **123**, 673.

EMERSON, R., CHALMERS, R. V. & CEDERSTRAND, C. N. (1957), 'Some factors influencing the long-wave limit of photosynthesis', *Proceedings of the National Academy of Sciences (USA)* **43**, 133–143.

FRANCK, J. (1949), 'An interpretation of the contradictory results in measurements of the photosynthetic quantum yield and related phenomena', *Archives of Biochemistry* **23**, 297–314.

FRANCK, J. & GAFFRON, H. (1941), 'Photosynthesis, facts and interpretation', *Advances in Enzymology* **1**, 199–262.

FRANCK, J. & HERZFELD, K. F. (1941), 'Contributions to a theory of photosynthesis', *Journal for Physical Chemistry* **45**, 978–1025.

FRANCK, J. & LOOMIS, W. E., Eds. (1949), *Photosynthesis in Plants*, Iowa State College Press, Ames, Iowa.

FRENCH, C. S. (1961), Light, Pigments and Photosynthesis, *in* W. D. McELROY & B. GLASS, Ed., 'Light and Life', The Johns Hopkins Press, Baltimore, pp. 447–474.

FRENCH, C. S. (1979), 'Fifty years of photosynthesis', *Annual Review of Plant Physiology* **30**, 1–26.

FRENKEL, A. W. (1993), 'Reflections', *Photosynthesis Research* **35**, 103–116.

FRUTON, J. S. (1999), *Proteins, Enzymes, Genes: The Interplay of Chemistry and Biology*, Yale University Press, New Haven / London.

GAFFRON, H. & WOHL, K. (1936), 'Zur Theorie der Assimilation', *Naturwissenschaften* **24**, 81–90; 103–107.

GAFFRON, H., BROWN, A. H., STACY, F. C., LIVINGSTON, R., RABINOWITCH, E. I., STREHLER, B. L. & TOLBERT, N. E., Eds. (1957), *Research in photosynthesis: papers and discussions presented at the Gatlinburg conference, October 25-29, 1955*, Interscience Publishers, Baltimore.

GEST, H. & BLANKENSHIP, R. E. (2004), 'Time line of discoveries: anoxygenic bacterial photosynthesis', *Photosynthesis Research* **80**, 59–70.

GOVINDJEE (1999), 'On the requirement of minimum number of four versus eight quanta of light for the evolution of one molecule of oxygen in photosynthesis: A historical note', *Photosynthesis Research* **59**, 249–254.

GOVINDJEE (2001), Lighting the Path: A Tribute to Robert Emerson (1903-1959), *in* 'PS2001: Proceedings, 12th International Congress on Photosynthesis, Brisbane, CSIRO'.

GOVINDJEE (2004), Robert Emerson and Eugene Rabinowitch: Understanding Photosynthesis, *in* L. HODDESON, Ed., 'No Boundaries: University of Illinois Vignettes', University of Illinois Press, Urbana/ Chicago, pp. 181–194.

GOVINDJEE (2010), 'Celebrating Andrew Alm Benson's 93rd birthday', *Photosynthesis Research* **105**, 201–208.

GOVINDJEE & BJÖRN, L. O. (2011), Dissecting Oxygenic Photosynthesis: The Evolution of the Z-Scheme for Thylakoid Membranes, *in* S. ITOH, P. MOHANTY & K. N. GURUPRASAD, Ed., 'Photosynthesis: Overviews on Recent Progress and Future Perspective', I. K. International Publishers, New Delhi, India, pp. 1–27.

GOVINDJEE & FORK, D. (2006), 'Charles Stacy French (1907-1995)', *Biographical Memoirs of the National Academy of Sciences* **88**, 1–29.

GOVINDJEE & KROGMANN, D. (2004), 'Discoveries in oxygenic photosynthesis (1727-2003): A perspective', *Photosynthesis Research* **80**, 15–27.

GOVINDJEE & RABINOWITCH, E. I. (1960), 'Two forms of chlorophyll *a* in vivo with distinct photochemical functions', *Science* **132**, 355–356.

GOVINDJEE, ALLEN, J. F. & BEATTY, J. T. (2004), 'Celebrating the millennium – historical highlights of photosynthesis research; Part 3', *Photosynthesis Research* **80**, 1–13.

GOVINDJEE, AMESZ, J. & KNOX, R. S. (1996*a*), 'Photosynthetic Unit: Antenna and Reaction Centers (Special issue dedicated to William Arnold)', Photosynthesis Research 48 (1-2).

GOVINDJEE, BEATTY, J. T., GEST, H. & ALLEN, J. F., Eds. (2005), *Discoveries in Photosynthesis*, Springer, Dordrecht.

GOVINDJEE, KNOX, R. S. & AMESZ, J. (1996*b*), 'Editorial (dedicated to William Arnold)', *Photosynthesis Research* **48**, 1–2.

GOVINDJEE, R., RABINOWITCH, E. I. & GOVINDJEE (1968), 'Maximum quantum yield and action spectra of photosynthesis and fluorescence in Chlorella', *Biochim. Biophys. Acta* **162**, 530–544.

GOVINDJEE, R., THOMAS, J. B. & RABINOWITCH, E. I. (1960), '"Second Emerson Effect" in the Hill reaction of Chlorella cells with quinone as oxidant', *Science* **132**, 421–421.

HAXO, F. T. & BLINKS, L. R. (1950), 'Photosynthetic action spectra of marine algae', *Journal of General Physiology* **33**, 389–421.

HENDRICKS, S. B. (1953), 'A discussion of photosynthesis', *Science* **117**, 370–373.

HENNING, E. (1987), Otto Heinrich Warburg – Der "Kaiser von Dahlem", *in* W. TREUE & G. HILDEBRANDT, Ed., 'Berlinische Lebensbilder. Bd. 1: Naturwissenschaftler', Colloquium Verlag, Berlin, pp. 299–316.

HENTSCHEL, K. (2005), *Die Mentalität deutscher Physiker in der frühen Nachkriegszeit (1945-1949)*, Synchron, Heidelberg.

HENTSCHEL, K., Ed. (1996), *Physics and National Socialism. An Anthology of Primary Sources*, Birkhäuser, Basel.

HERRON, H. A. (1996), 'About Bill Arnold, my father', *Photosynthesis Research* **48**, 3–7.

HILL, R. & WHITTINGHAM, C. P. (1955), *Photosynthesis*, John Wiley, New York.

HOMANN, P. H. (2005), Hydrogen meatbolism of green algae: discovery and early research – a tribute to Hans Gaffron and his coworkers, *in* GOVINDJEE, J. T. BEATTY, H. GEST & J. ALLEN, Ed., 'Discoveries in Photosynthesis', Springer, Dordrecht, pp. 119–129.

HOPPE, B. (1997), Structural Development of Experimental Methods in the Researches on Gas-Exchange and Photosynthesis, *in* B. HOPPE, Ed., 'Biology Integrating Scientific Fundamentals: Contributions to the History of Interrelations between Biology, Chemistry, and Physics from the 18th to the 20th Centuries', Bd. 21 von *Algorismus: Studien zur Geschichte der Mathematik und der Naturwissenschaften*, Institut für Geschichte der Naturwissenschaften, München, pp. 10–30.

HUGHES, J. (2003), *The Manhattan Project: Big Science and the Atom Bomb*, Columbia University Press.

HUZISIGE, H. & KE, B. (1993), 'Dynamics of the history of photosynthesis research', *Photosynthesis Research* **38**, 185–209.

HÖXTERMANN, E. (1992), 'Fundamental discoveries in the history of photosynthesis research', *Photosynthetica* **26**, 485–502.

HÖXTERMANN, E. (2001), Otto Heinrich Warburg (1883-1970), *in* I. JAHN & M. SCHMITT, Ed., 'Darwin & Co. Eine Geschichte der Biologie in Portraits. Vol. 2', Beck, München, pp. 251–274.

HÖXTERMANN, E. (2007), 'A comment on Warburg's early understanding of biocatalysis', *Photosynthesis Research* **92**, 121–127.

HÖXTERMANN, E. & SUCKER, U. (1989), *Otto Warburg*, Biographien hervorragender Naturwissenschaftler, Techniker und Mediziner; 91, Teubner, Leipzig.

KAMEN, M. D. (1985), *Radiant Science, Dark Politics. A Memoir of the Nuclear Age*, University of California Press, Berkeley.

KELLY, C. C., Ed. (2007), *The Manhattan Project: The birth of the atomic bomb in the words of its creators, eyewitnesses, and historians*, Black Dog & Leventhal.

KOHLER, R. E. (1973), 'The background to Otto Warburg's conception of the Atmungsferment', *Journal of the History of Biology* **6**(2), 171–192.

KOK, B. (1960), Efficiency of Photosynthesis, *in* A. PIRSON, Ed., 'Handbuch der Pflanzenphysiologie', Springer, Berlin/ Göttingen/ Heidelberg, pp. 566–633.

KREBS, H. (1979), *Otto Warburg: Zellphysiologe, Biochemiker, Mediziner 1883-1970*, Grosse Naturforscher; 41, Wissenschaftliche Verlagsgesellschaft, Stuttgart.

LEMMERICH, J. (2007), *Aufrecht im Sturm der Zeit: Der Physiker James Franck (1882-1964)*, Verlag für Geschichte der Naturwissenschaften und Technik, Diepholz / Stuttgart / Berlin.

LEY, A. & MAUZERALL, D. (1982), 'Absolute absorption cross-sections for photosystem II and the quantum requirement for photosynthesis in Chlorella vulgaris', *Biochim. Biophys. Acta* **680**, 95–106.

LICHTENTHALER, H. K., BUCHANAN, B. B. & DOUCE, R. (2008), 'Honoring Andrew Benson in Paris: A tribute on his 90th birthday', *Photosynthesis Research* **96**, 181–183.

LINEWEAVER, H. & BURK, D. (1934), 'The determination of enzyme dissociation constants', *Journal of the American Chemical Society* **56**, 658–666.

LOOMIS, W. E. (1960), Historical Introduction, *in* A. PIRSON & W. RUHLAND, Ed., 'Handbuch der Pflanzenphysiologie', Bd. 5, 1, Springer, Berlin / Göttingen / Heidelberg, pp. 85–114.

MACRAKIS, K. (1993), *Surviving the Swastika. Scientific Research in Nazi Germany*, Oxford University Press, New York / Oxford.

MAGEE, J. L., DE WITT, T. W., SMITH, E. C. & DANIELS, F. (1939), 'A photocalorimeter. The quantum efficiency of photosynthesis in algae', *Journal of the American Chemical Society* **61**, 3529–3533.

MANNING, W. M., STAUFFER, J. F., DUGGAR, B. M. & DANIELS, F. (1938), 'Quantum efficiency of photosynthesis in *Chlorella*', *Journal of the American Chemical Society* **60**, 266–274.

MYERS, J. (1974), 'Conceptual developments in photosynthesis', *Plant Physiology* **54**, 420–426.

NG, K.-S. & BASSHAM, J. A. (1968), 'The quantum requirement of photosynthesis in Chlorella', *Biochim. Biophys. Acta* **162**, 254–264.

NICKELSEN, K. (2007), 'Otto Warburg's first approach to photosynthesis', *Photosynthesis Research* **92**, 109–120.

NICKELSEN, K. (2008*a*), 'Ein bisher unbekanntes Zeitzeugnis – Otto Warburgs Tagebuchnotizen Feb.-April 1945', *NTM* **16**, 103–115.

NICKELSEN, K. (2008*b*), 'From leaves to molecules: Botany and the development of photosynthesis research', *Annals for the History and Philosophy of Biology* **12**, 1–40.

NICKELSEN, K. (2009*a*), 'The construction of a scientific model: Otto Warburg and the Building Block Strategy', *Studies in History and Philosophy of Biological and Biomedical Sciences* **40**, 73–86.

NICKELSEN, K. (2009*b*), *Of Light and Darkness: Modelling Photosynthesis 1840-1960*, Habilitation; submitted to the Faculty of Sciences of the University of Bern, October 2009, Bern.

NICKELSEN, K. & GRASSHOFF, G. (IN PRESS, 2011), 'In pursuit of formaldehyde: causally explanatory models and falsification', *Studies in History and Philosophy of Biological and Biomedical Sciences*.

NISHIMURA, M. S., EMERSON, R., HATA, T. & KAGEYAMA, A. (1944), 'The propagation of guayule from cuttings', *American Journal of Botany* **31**, 412–418.

NISHIMURA, M. S., HIROSAWA, F. N. & EMERSON, R. (1947), 'Rubber from Guayule', *Industrial and Engineering Chemistry* **39**, 1477–1485.

NISHIMURA, M. S., WHITTINGHAM, C. P. & EMERSON, R. (1951), The Maximum Efficiency of Photosynthesis, *in* 'Carbon Dioxide Fixation and Photosynthesis', Cambridge University Press, pp. 176–210.

PIRSON, A. (1994), 'Sixty years in algal physiology and photosynthesis', *Photosynthesis Research* **40**, 207–221.

PIRSON, A., KROLLPFEIFFER, I. & SCHAEFER, G. (1953), 'Leistungsfähigkeit und Fehlerquellen manometrischer Stoffwechselmessungen', *Marburger Sitzungsberichte* **76**, 3–27.

RABINOWITCH, A. (2005), 'Founder and father', *Bulletin of the Atomic Scientists* **61**, 30–37.

RABINOWITCH, E. I. (1945), *Photosynthesis and Related Processes. Vol I: Chemistry of Photosynthesis, Chemosynthesis and Related Processes in Vitro and in Vivo*, Interscience Publishers, New York.

RABINOWITCH, E. I. (1948), 'Photosynthesis', *Scientific American* **179**, 24–35.

RABINOWITCH, E. I. (1951), *Photosynthesis and Related Processes. Vol II, 1: Spectroscopy and Fluorescence of Photosynthetic Pigments; Kinetics of Photosynthesis*, Interscience Publishers, New York.

RABINOWITCH, E. I. (1956), *Photosynthesis and Related Processes. Vol II, 2: Kinetics of Photosynthesis (continued); Addenda*, Interscience Publishers, New York.

RABINOWITCH, E. I. (1959), 'Robert Emerson, 1903-1959', *Plant Physiology* **34**, 179–184.

RABINOWITCH, E. I. (1961), 'Robert Emerson (1903-1959)', *Biographical Memoirs of the National Academy of Sciences* **25**, 112–131.

RABINOWITCH, E. I. & GOVINDJEE (1961), Different Forms of Chlorophyll *a* in vivo and their Photochemical Function, *in* W. D. MCELROY & B. GLASS, Ed., 'Light and Life', Johns Hopkins Press, Baltimore, pp. 378–386.

RABINOWITCH, E. I. & GOVINDJEE (1969), *Photosynthesis*, John Wiley & Sons, New York/London/Sydney/Toronto. (Available free at: http://www.life.illinois.edu/govindjee/photosynBook.html).

RIEKE, F. F. (1939), 'On the quantum efficiency of photosynthesis', *Journal of Chemical Physics* **7**, 238–244.

RIEKE, F. F. (1949), Quantum Efficiencies for Photosynthesis and Photoreduction in Green Plants, *in* J. FRANCK & W. E. LOOMIS, Ed., 'Photosynthesis in Plants', Iowa State College Press, Ames, Iowa, pp. 251–272.

ROSENBERG, J. L. (2004), 'The contributions of James Franck to photosynthesis research: a tribute', *Photosynthesis Research* **80**, 71–76.

RÜSKAMP, W., Ed. (1989), *Eine vollkommene Närrin durch meine ewigen Gefühle. Aus den Tagebüchern der Lotte Warburg 1925 bis 1947*, Druckhaus Bayreuth.

SKILLMAN, J. (2008), 'Quantum yield variation across the three pathways of photosynthesis: not yet out of the dark', *Journal of Experimental Botany* **59**, 1647–1661.

STEMLER, A. J. (2002), 'The bicarbonate effect, oxygen evolution, and the shadow of Otto Warburg', *Photosynthesis Research* **73**(73), 177–183.

THORHAUG, A. & BERLYN, G. (2009), 'A tribute to Lawrence Rogers Blinks (1900-1989): light and algae', *Photosynthesis Research* **100**, 129–141.

VAN RENSEN, J. J. S., XU, C. & GOVINDJEE (1999), 'Role of bicarbonate in the photosystem II, the water-plastoquinone oxido-reductase of plant photosynthesis', *Physiologia Plantarum* **105**, 585–592.

VENNESLAND, B. (1981), 'Reflections and small confessions', *Annual Reviews of Plant Physiology* **32**, 1–20.

WALKER, D. (1992), *Energy, Plants and Man*, Oxygraphics Limited.

WALKER, D. (1997), 'Tell me where all past years are', *Photosynthesis Research* **51**, 1–26.

WARBURG, O. (1919), 'Über die Geschwindigkeit der photochemischen Kohlensäurezersetzung in lebenden Zellen I', *Biochemische Zeitschrift* **100**, 230–270.

WARBURG, O. (1920), 'Über die Geschwindigkeit der photochemischen Kohlensäurezersetzung in lebenden Zellen. II.', *Biochemische Zeitschrift* **103**, 188–217.

WARBURG, O. (1921), 'Theorie der Kohlensäureassimilation', *Naturwissenschaften* **9**, 354–358.

WARBURG, O. (1945), 'Über den Quantenbedarf der Kohlensäureassimilation', *Naturwissenschaften* **33**, 122–122.

WARBURG, O. (1948), 'Assimilatory quotient and photochemical yield', *American Journal of Botany* **35**, 194–204.

WARBURG, O. (1951), 'Ein-Quantenmechanismus der Photosynthese', *Angewandte Chemie* **63**, 282–283.

WARBURG, O. (1952), 'Energetik und Photosynthese', *Naturwissenschaften* **39**, 337–341.

WARBURG, O. (1958), 'Photosynthesis. Experiments at the Max Planck Institute for Cell Physiology, Berlin-Dahlem', *Science* **128**(3315), 68–73.

WARBURG, O. & BURK, D. (1950*a*), '1-Quanten-Mechanismus und Energie-Kreisprozess bei der Photosynthese', *Naturwissenschaften* **37**, 560.

WARBURG, O. & BURK, D. (1950*b*), 'The maximum efficiency of photosynthesis', *Archives of Biochemistry* **25**, 410–443.

WARBURG, O. & KRIPPAHL, G. (1958), 'Hill-Reaktionen', *Zeitschrift für Naturforschung B* **13**, 509–514.

WARBURG, O. & NEGELEIN, E. (1922), 'Über den Energieumsatz bei der Kohlensäureassimilation', *Zeitschrift für Physikalische Chemie* **102**, 235–266.

WARBURG, O. & NEGELEIN, E. (1923), 'Über den Einfluss der Wellenlänge auf den Energieumsatz bei der Kohlensäureassimilation', *Zeitschrift für Physikalische Chemie* **106**, 191–218.

WARBURG, O., BURK, D., SCHOCKEN, V. & HENDRICKS, S. (1950), 'The quantum efficiency of photosynthesis', *Biochim. Biophys. Acta* **4**, 335–349.

WARBURG, O., GELEICK, H. & BRIESE, K. (1952), 'Über die Messung der Photosynthese in Carbonat-Bicarbonat-Gemischen', *Zeitschrift für Naturforschung* **7b**, 141.

WARBURG, O., KRIPPAHL, G. & LEHMAN, A. (1969), 'Chlorophyll catalysis and Einstein's law of photochemical equivalence in photosynthesis', *American Journal of Botany* **56**, 961–971.

WARBURG, O., KRIPPAHL, G. & SCHRÖDER, W. (1954), 'Katalytische Wirkung des blaugrünen Lichts auf den Energieumsatz bei der Photosynthese', *Zeitschrift für Naturforschung* **9b**, 667–675.

WARBURG, O., KRIPPAHL, G. & SCHRÖDER, W. (1955), 'Wirkungsspektrum eines Photosynthese-Fermentes', *Zeitschrift für Naturforschung* **10b**, 631–639.

WARBURG, O., KRIPPAHL, G. & SCHRÖDER, W. (1956), 'Über den chemischen Mechanismus der Kohlesäureassimilation', *Naturwissenschaften* **43**, 237–241.

WERNER, P. (1991), *Ein Genie irrt seltener. Otto Heinrich Warburg, ein Lebensbild in Dokumenten*, Akademie Verlag, Berlin.

138

WERNER, P. (1996), *Otto Warburgs Beitrag zur Atmungstheorie: Das Problem der Sauerstoffaktivierung*, Basiliskenpresse, Marburg.

WILLSTÄTTER, R. & STOLL, A. (1918), *Untersuchungen über die Assimilation der Kohlensäure. Sieben Abhandlungen*, Springer, Berlin.

WITT, H. T. (1991), 'Functional mechanism of water splitting photosynthesis', *Photosynthesis Research* **29**, 55–77.

ZALLEN, D. T. (1993), 'The "light" organism for the job: Green algae and photosynthesis research', *Journal of the History of Biology* **26**, 269–279.